Praise for Michael Geraghty

"Thanks for the really excellent negotiation presentation at our National Salesperson's Meeting at Lake Lanier, Georgia. I was so impressed personally that I would like to invite you to make a similar one to our regional managers in San Francisco."

—Peter Schultz, president, Heraeus Amersil, Duluth, Georgia

"Thanks for a great job. Your keynote on sales negotiation at our worldwide sales conference in Austin, Texas, was very well received."

—Roger Minard, CEO, Austin Semiconductor

"My vice president of sales told me that in twenty years of attending presentations, yours was the finest he had heard."

—Tim Johnson, CEO, Natus, San Carlos, California

"Your negotiation presentations in Boulder, Colorado, at our national sales conference were excellent."

—Mark Stevenson, CEO, Electronic Manufacturing Systems

"A masterful keynote on negotiation if ever there was one! Not only that, but glowing reports continue to come in about your negotiation workshops. We are in your debt for adding immeasurably to the success of the conference at Notre Dame University, Indiana."

—**John Flynn,** president, International Union of Bricklayers and Craft workers

"Occasionally a speaker comes your way and you have the urge to contact other program directors to advise them of the excellent program you had just witnessed. Michael Geraghty had us spellbound with his presentation."

—**Fred Marcussen,** president, Wright, Marcussen, and Kirby

"You have a rare ability to communicate with people."

—**Fred Solish**, CEO, eParagon

"Your sense of humor, your excellent communication skills with the audience, and your mastery of the subject of negotiation kept our large turnout riveted to the presentation—quite a feat."

—**Bob Peterson,** VP, Oracle Corporation

"Your negotiation keynote at our worldwide sales conference in Orlando, Florida, was very informative and helpful to our entire group. The feedback I received was very positive."

—**Wayne Steinhoff**, VP, marketing and sales, Osram Sylvania

Anybody Can Negotiate—Even You!

Anybody Can Negotiate—Even You!

♦

How to Become a Master Negotiator

Michael Geraghty

iUniverse, Inc.
New York Lincoln Shanghai

Anybody Can Negotiate—Even You!
How to Become a Master Negotiator

iUniverse books may be ordered through booksellers or by contacting:

iUniverse
2021 Pine Lake Road, Suite 100
Lincoln, NE 68512
www.iuniverse.com
1-800-Authors (1-800-288-4677)

ISBN-13: 978-0-595-36466-4 (pbk)
ISBN-13: 978-0-595-80898-4 (ebk)
ISBN-10: 0-595-36466-7 (pbk)
ISBN-10: 0-595-80898-0 (ebk)

Printed in the United States of America

Who are the best negotiators in the world? I have often asked that question in my workshops all over America. I often hear these answers—the Chinese, the Japanese, the French, the English, the Brazilians, and the Americans. In my opinion the best negotiators on the planet are kids! Kids are terrific negotiators for two reasons:

- They do not understand the meaning of the word no.

- They are very persistent. "But Dad, everybody else is doing it."

This book is dedicated to three terrific negotiators—my three beautiful daughters, who continually keep me on my toes and continue to teach me much about negotiation.

Kathryn Kelly Geraghty   Born 2/16/85
Clare Kennedy Geraghty   Born 10/26/89
Anne Frances Geraghty   Born 5/21/94

And to the memory of my parents:

William Patrick Geraghty   1905–1994
Lilian Kennedy Geraghty   1911–1983

"Michael Geraghty is a master storyteller."

—IBM Corporation

"Michael Geraghty is a master of negotiation."

—Oracle Corporation

Contents

Acknowledgments

This book is the product of over twenty years of direct involvement in thousands of negotiations all over the world. During that time I have had the privilege of observing and dealing with some of the best negotiators on the planet and also some of the worst. As a result, I developed a very simple philosophy of negotiation:

• Watch what successful negotiators do and do it.

• Observe what poor negotiators do and make sure you avoid it.

During that time I read many books and articles on negotiation. I realize I stand on the shoulders of many negotiators who have gone before me. You may notice I have not referenced many texts to support the many ideas in this book. The reason is simple. I wanted to write a book on negotiation that anybody can understand. This book is not for the experts. It is meant for the ordinary person like you, who is thirsty for knowledge and would like to become a master of persuasion.

I have been very fortunate in that throughout much of my career I have had excellent mentors. I met only a few of them physically. That's the great thing about them. Through books, tapes, and videos I have received excellent advice. In America, I would like here to pay tribute to Brian Tracy, Jim Rohm, Earl Nightingale, Dennis Waitley, Clement Stone, and Napoleon Hill—also to Somers White from Phoenix, Arizona, a wonderful consultant and true friend.

I want to also acknowledge the thousands of students who have attended my workshops over the past ten years. Some of their ideas and insights appear on the pages of this book.

Finally, I want to thank my daughter Kathryn for her invaluable ideas and suggestions during the final edit of this book.

1

Setting the Negotiation Stage

Negotiation is the "art of friendly persuasion." It is "the ability to sell yourself and your ideas." Study after study reveals that negotiation is one of the top three skills in life and on the job. Great negotiators become key contributors to any company or organization. Great negotiators know exactly what they want and exactly how to get it. Their communication during negotiations is crisp, clear, and concise. When difficulties arise during negotiations, they have the ability to make the necessary adjustments to achieve winning solutions.

In this book, you will gain a great understanding of the psychology of negotiation and develop powerful skills to ensure your success. You can become a terrific negotiator if you learn the rules of the negotiation game. Negotiation is like a chess game. You must learn the rules of the game. When you do, you will become a master negotiator.

• This book will help you discover the negotiation genius inside yourself.

How You Can Make the Most of This Book

I have conducted countless negotiation workshops all over America, for corporations like Motorola and Cisco, for labor unions, for accountants, for salespeople, and for buyers. The procedures, techniques, and ideas I will describe here in detail have worked not only for me but also for countless others. Many of them will need alteration or adaptation to your own negotiation needs. Therefore you should often ask this question as you read this book:

• *How can I adapt this information to fit my situation?*

As you read, you and I are going to be involved in a learning and motivational experience that will enable you to be a far more effective negotiator. My major objective is to get you heavily involved in the learning-and-doing process that will

1

take place, as you take in all the ideas and tips. Think about what you read, try to understand it, and, above all, decide to take action as soon as possible. The advice I will share with you in the course of this book has the potential to make you a superb negotiator. But the missing ingredient is you, and your ability and desire to take action. Therefore this question is most important—what are you going to do with the information you will receive? That is the bottom line. I will remind you of this again in the last chapter of this book.

What is the most frustrating experience of a salesperson? It is when the prospect says yes to all the questions the salesperson asks, except the last one. "Is the product good?" "Yes." Will the product save you money?" "Yes." "Do you need it?" "Yes." "Would you like to have it?" "Yes." "Can you afford it?" "Yes." "Are you going to buy it?" "No." What has happened here is that the prospect has been convinced but has not been persuaded to take action. I want you to know that I will be persuading you to take action throughout this book. How will I be doing this?

As you read, you will be hearing key stories. You will be asked questions. All the surveys tell us that the very best communicators use two key skills—they tell wonderful stories, and they ask the right questions. I am basically a storyteller. I grew up in a tiny village in Ireland, and, as a kid, I listened to endless stories. Two of the greatest speakers in history came from Italy and Greece. Cicero was a Roman senator who lived just before Christ and gave superb speeches. When he finished speaking in the Roman Senate, people said, "Wasn't that a wonderful speech?" Centuries before Cicero, Demosthenes lived in Greece. He first had to overcome a terrible stutter. He would practice speeches by the ocean and would do a very strange thing—he'd place pebbles in his mouth, and he would speak to the rolling waves. Then he would take the pebbles out of his mouth and would speak again to the rolling waves—in his own mind he sounded much better. Eventually he became a magnificent speaker.

In those days, war was common. Whenever the king of Greece wanted to get his troops ready for war he would give the order, "Bring in Demosthenes to speak to my soldiers." After he spoke, the soldiers did not say, "Wasn't that a fantastic speech?" They simply said, "We are now ready to march. We are ready for war."

I have a very important two-part question for you—what was the difference between Cicero and Demosthenes, and why is it so important for you? The difference was that Cicero was in the business of presentation, whereas Demosthenes was in the business of persuasion. There is a huge difference. I'm all for Cicero, but negotiators are in the business of persuasion and so are you.

Get ready to march! You can become a terrific negotiator if you really want to. This book will give you all the tools you need to become a terrific negotiator. You already have within you everything it takes to make a great success of your life. My mission in this book is very simple—to wake up the negotiation genius inside you. Thanks for the pleasure of your company as we travel along this wonderful journey together. I love to join people on their journey, and transfer skills. I am sure you can teach me many things. I am also sure I can teach you to become a great negotiator. Let's enjoy our journey together and make the most of it.

Three Key Skills in Life and in Negotiation

In my workshops, I am often asked this question: what are the top three skills negotiators need for the twenty-first century? Here they are:

- Deal effectively with adversity

- Communicate clearly

- Persuade successfully

Deal Effectively with Adversity

Consider the story of Mrs. Mulligan. Every year I return to Ireland. I always go back to the village I grew up in, and I always visit the graves of my parents. Buried next to my mother is Mrs. Mulligan. She "died" twice! That's a very strange thing to say, isn't it? How can a person die twice? What do you think I mean by that? Let me explain. Mrs. Mulligan physically died in 1993 and she was buried; however, she really died psychologically in 1979, and this is how she died: in that year, just before Christmas, her sixteen-year-old son, Edward, was killed in a car crash. He had just breakfasted with his mom, kissed her, and said, "I love you," before going off to school. Two hours later, Mrs. Mulligan heard the terrible news that she would never see her son again. That was the day she really "died." Yes, she did physically live another fourteen years, but mentally and psychologically, she was in another place. She went into a deep dark dungeon of depression and never came out. I am not being critical of Mrs. Mulligan—perhaps she was too sensitive.

However, all my life I have been fascinated by this question—why are some people able to handle adversity much better than others? Two people hear the same news, "Your son has been killed," and both go through the same grief. Both of them are devastated. However, one stays devastated and does not come out of it. The other goes into a state of black depression but eventually comes out of it and goes on to live a very fruitful life. What's the difference that makes the difference? Hemingway has a wonderful quote: "The world breaks everybody, and afterwards some are strong in the broken places."

I believe that one of them is able to cope with adversity, and the other is not able to cope. And we all know people like that, don't we? We all know drug addicts who never come out of the gutter, whereas others do, and go on to lead very positive lives. We all know alcoholics who do the same—get their lives back on track, while others remain stuck.

That is why I believe the skill of dealing with adversity is one of the great skills in negotiation as well as in life and why we need great role models to help us. Henry Ford had it right: "If you think you can, or if you think you can't, you're right!" He walked the talk. Did you know that he went bankrupt three times in his career before coming back to make it big financially? Think about that for a moment. It's bad enough to go bankrupt once. Most people don't come back from that. It is very hard to handle. Then you repeat the traumatic experience not just once but two more times, as Ford did. What was inside him that made him come back three times from bankruptcy before finally hitting it big financially? Do you think he was able to deal effectively with adversity?

The old saying is true: "What happens to you is not half as important as how you react to what happens to you." Be very careful what you say to yourself when you experience a failure. Some people fail and say to themselves, *I am a failure.* Others go through the same experience and say, *I now know how not to do it next time around. This failure has been a terrific learning experience.*

What has all this got to do with negotiation? Everything. Negotiations can be very stressful and full of adversity—sometimes there can be confrontation, hostility, and anger. The negotiators who can handle adversity always have a winning edge.

Winston Churchill is one of my heroes. That surprises people because he is English and I am Irish, and the history between our two countries has not always been positive. I admire him tremendously for a few different reasons. He enjoyed his drink, and he had a great sense of humor. As a young man he had a stutter, yet went on to become a brilliant public speaker. He also suffered badly from depression, which he called the *Black Dogs*. Most of all he had a bulldog determination, especially when things were not going well. In a very tough time for England during World War II, he kept the spirit of England upbeat. He once said this:

- "I can sum up my life in seven words. Never give up. Never, never, give up."

- Persistence in the face of adversity is a terrific skill in life—and in negotiation.

Communicate Clearly

We all communicate, but how many of us communicate with total clarity? Surveys reveal that less than 20 percent of people communicate with total clarity. Note that I am talking here not so much about communication but instead about clarity when we communicate. Lack of clarity in communication causes huge complications in relationships, and it causes huge complications in corporate America.

What is the divorce rate in America right now? The national average is 50 percent. In California it is 58 percent and rising. What is the number one reason for divorce in America? I would have thought the answer to that question was simple—"money." I would have answered wrong—turns out that money is down on the list. The real answer is poor communication skills. Divorcees put it more strongly: "Lousy communication skills ruined our marriage and caused our divorce."

So, if "lousy communication skills" cause big problems in marriages, you don't need to be an Einstein to figure out that "lousy communication skills" cause big problems in the workplace. Have you ever been at work and someone phones you? Three minutes into the conversation you are saying to yourself, "What exactly is your point? I don't have time to guess what you are looking for; can you cut to the chase?" That is what you are thinking internally, but externally you are getting impatient and frustrated. Did you know that key managers at Sun Microsystems average 250 e-mails a day because they have to be copied on all kinds of projects? I asked one of these managers, "What is your pet peeve at work?" She replied, "Trying to guess what exactly people are saying in their e-mails. Lack of clarity drives me crazy."

Therefore, J.D. Rockefeller got it right: "I will pay more for the ability to communicate clearly and get on well with others than for any other ability under the sun." And he ought to know what he was talking about. Want to hear what Paul Getty once said? "I would gladly have given up one of my billions to have made one of my marriages work!"

Over the years I have had the privilege of hearing some of the best professional speakers in America. The top speakers work extremely hard on clarity. They are crisp, precise, and crystal clear. Great negotiators are the same. They work very hard at making sure they are crystal clear during each stage of the negotiations. The great ones often say, "Let me understand what I think you said, to your satisfaction." They are always looking for feedback to ensure clarity. They ask high-performance questions to get the key information they need.

Persuade Successfully

We all know people who can sell sand in the desert. We also know people who could not sell water in the desert, don't we? Some are very persuasive and others need to work hard on it. Recently I was reading a political book and was fascinated with the following vignette. In all political parties you have some people who are so good at persuasion that the only job they do is to persuade very rich people to contribute 100 *thousand* dollars to the Republicans or to the Democrats. How would you go about this? Would you like to know how one extremely persuasive person did it? He was asked to target people whose net worth was in excess of 100 million dollars. Can you imagine that the 400th person on the *Forbes* list of 2005's wealthiest Americans has a net worth of $900 million? This is what he would say to these high rollers: "Would you prefer to keep all 100 million dollars, or still have 99.9 million, fly on the candidate's airplane, campaign with him, and if he's elected have access to the President and be invited to the White House?" Know what this very smart persuader said? "You'd be surprised how many wrote checks for 100 thousand dollars when it was put to them that way!"

Think about it—most of us spend most of our life in the business of persuasion. Persuading our boss that we do a good job. Persuading our kids to behave responsibly. Persuading highway patrol not to give us a ticket. Trying to sell our ideas to upper management. Think back over all the conversations you've had in the past year, and you may be amazed to discover how many of them involved persuasion.

Not too long ago I was having a coffee in a Starbucks in San Francisco. I was seated on a stool looking out at what was happening in front of my eyes. I observed two people hustling for money. One looked as if he was strung out on drugs and was aggressive. Do you think he got money? No, because people were avoiding him. Across the street I observed another man; he was seated on the ground, with his eyes facing downward. He looked like he needed a good meal. Beside him was a handwritten notice saying, "Please give if you want to. Thank you." Do you think he got money, and why? Yes he did. I was fascinated to see some people rushing by, and then stopping for a moment and going back to give him money. I saw him getting some dollar bills. Both these people were in the business of persuasion, one was doing it wrong with an aggressive approach, whereas the other was doing fine with a more persuasive approach. So if you ever need some extra money, do I have a job for you on the streets of San Francisco!

That's what negotiation is—it is the art of friendly persuasion. And it is a learned skill. Anybody can become a fabulous negotiator, if you get the proper training. It is just like learning to ride a bike or drive a car. I will never forget the first time getting into a car with a stick shift. I knew immediately I had a huge problem. Three pedals but only two feet. I thought I would never master the art of using those three pedals with my two feet. Now I get into a car and it is effortless; I do it without even thinking. The same applies to negotiation. Right now you may think you could never master the craft of persuasion. Think again. This book will help you change that attitude. Start thinking, "I can become a great negotiator if I really want to. All I need is some proper training." That is what this book is all about.

I will be sharing with you lessons I have learned along the negotiation journey, as well as mistakes I have made. I must tell you that some of my best learning experiences in negotiation have been from my biggest mistakes. In many ways I failed my way to success as a negotiator.

Why Should You Listen To Me?

I spent fifteen years working for a Fortune 500 company in Silicon Valley. The company manufactured mainframe computers. What is a mainframe computer? It's the second largest computer a company can buy. Ever wonder about the technology behind Bank of America's ATM machines? Wonder no more—chances are very good they are powered by one of our mainframe computers. Ever wonder about American Airlines' state-of-the-art reservation systems? Wonder no more because mainframe computers, either the competition's or ours, also power them. In the 1980s a lower-end mainframe computer would cost you about $2 million, whereas one with all the bells and whistles could cost $18 million.

Sixteen Seconds on the Information Superhighway

To give you a feeling of the world of mainframe computers, suppose you and your significant other decide to go to Paris, France, for a nice romantic vacation. Now imagine you have an ATM card that worked all over the world, including Paris. Let me take you by the hand and bring you on a fascinating sixteen-second journey along the information superhighway, at electronic speeds.

You pop that card into the ATM machine in Paris, and suddenly an amazing thing happens. The mainframe computer running that ATM says to itself, *This is not a French ATM card.* No big deal you may say, but it really is a big deal because in a split second, faster than you can blink your eye, that computer has determined that of the fifty-eight million French consumers, you are not one of them! The computer then gives an order, *Go into the European network and see if this is a European card.* Once again, at electronic speeds, the computer faithfully executes this command. Of the 338 million European consumers, it has figured you are not one of them, and it has done this at astonishing speeds. Finally the last order is given: *This is not a European card, go into the global network and see where it comes from.* This is where the fun begins, along with the astonishing numbers.

How many people presently inhabit planet Earth? The number may astound you—it is presently about 6.3 billion. Of those 6.3 billion, suppose 60% hold credit cards. The computer is saying, *This card is not Brazilian, Australian, Chinese—it is an American card.* Once again at mind-numbing speed, it goes into the American network, and of the 180 million American consumers, it figures out that your ATM card is from San Francisco, California. It then goes into your bank account and determines you are good for the amount you want. All of the above can take sixteen seconds, and then out comes your money in French Euros. Welcome to the world of mainframe computers.

This was my world for fifteen years and a fascinating world it was. For years I negotiated the prices for parts and assemblies that make up these computers. I had a group of fourteen buyers working for me, with a budget of about $250 million a year. So in any four-year period, I was intimately involved in business negotiations of over a billion dollars.

During those years I had the opportunity to study and observe some of the best negotiators in the world and also some of the worst. As a result, I developed a very simple philosophy of success:

• Watch what successful people do and do it.

• Observe what failures do and avoid it.

It's the same with negotiation.

• Watch what successful negotiators do and do it.

• Observe what poor negotiators do and avoid it.

In this book I will be sharing with you some of the things I learned along the way.

Notice what I have just tried to do—I tried to sell myself to you regarding my credibility, and hopefully I have succeeded. The bigger and far more important point is that you, dear reader, will also have to do the very same in all kinds of situations. You will have to "sell" yourself and your ideas and persuade others to "buy" them. And the best of luck to you!

Key Points

• This book will help you discover the negotiation genius inside yourself.

• Surveys tell us the best communicators use two key skills—they tell wonderful stories and they ask the right questions. The best negotiators are the best communicators.

• The best negotiators deal effectively with adversity: they communicate clearly, and they persuade successfully.

• Most of us spend our lives in the business of persuasion: persuading our boss that we do a good job, persuading our kids to behave responsibly, trying to sell our ideas to upper management. We better become pretty good persuaders.

• Start thinking *I can become a master negotiator if I really want to.* All the tools you need are in this book.

• "If you think you can or if you think you can't—you're correct."—Henry Ford.

2

A Drama with
Four Amazing Characters

Negotiation is a drama with these four amazing characters called power, information, time, and the iceberg. During this drama these characters make their entrances and their exits. Sometimes the spotlight is on one of them, and at other times the spotlight is on two of them. Occasionally, they are all on center stage, but they are all making their exits and entrances during the course of the negotiations. I want you to get to know these characters because the more you get to know them, the better the negotiator you will become.

To illustrate, consider this very simple example. Perhaps you never thought of it like this before. You are driving at seventy-seven miles an hour in a sixty-five miles an hour driving zone. Suddenly this red light starts flashing behind you. Yikes, it's highway patrol. Suddenly the curtain opens, and a drama is about to take place, and you have a starring role. How are you going to play it?

Power

The starring role here is an awesome character called power. I have a question for you. Who has the power role in this exciting drama—you or the officer? Interesting question isn't it? Many drivers think, *Oh, poor little me, I have no power. The officer has all the power, and I have none.* If that is what you think, welcome to the club. Studies reveal that many negotiators always think the other side has far more power than they do. I do a lot of workshops for salespeople. "Who has more power," I ask them, "you or the buyers?" "The buyers, of course," they say, "because they issue the purchase orders." I also do workshops for buyers. "Who has more power," I ask them, "you or the salespeople?" "The salespeople, because they can go above our heads if we say no." Most people, including drivers, think the other side has more power.

11

Information

Information is a critical character here. The officer has a key piece of information about you—you were actually driving seventy-seven miles an hour—it's right there on the radar gun. You argue with the officer, "Officer, I could not have been doing seventy-seven miles an hour." "Ma'am, look at the number here on the radar gun, what does it say?" Sure enough, you sheepishly have to admit that the information the officer has is correct. Note how powerful this character called information is. You may doubt it, you may go to court and fight it, but as soon as the judge is introduced to this information character in the form of seventy-seven MPH, you are toast.

Time

The character called time is important as well. You have about fifteen seconds to persuade the officer to give you a break. How is that? Simple—you dare not allow the officer to write down the first letter of your first name. The reason is that if he does that, he has to complete the ticket. You are under big time pressure here, so you have to act quickly to either distract the officer or persuade him to give you a break. Fifteen seconds is not very long to do that, but the character called time is also powerful.

Iceberg

The iceberg character is also fascinating in this drama. The iceberg means the power of personalization. Is there some way you can make the officer identify with you? Can you establish rapport? Understanding this aspect is critical for you, if you want to increase your powers of persuasion. I have an Irish accent, so it becomes extra heavy when highway patrol pulls me over. What am I doing? I am trying to portray myself as a foreigner hoping the officer may look at me more kindly. Anything you can do to make people identify with you will give you an edge. We will return later to this critical aspect of negotiation.

Welcome to the wonderful world of negotiations. Whether you are dealing with highway patrol, buying a house, interviewing for a job, negotiating for a raise, fighting a bank over overdraft fees, or persuading a mate to marry you, these four characters called power, information, time, and the iceberg will always be there. This book will make you very familiar with each of them. Remember, the more familiar you become with each of them, the better negotiator you are going to be.

By the way, last year I was conducting a workshop near Sacramento, California. Among my students were six highway patrol officers. They told me that tickets are negotiable if the driver handles it correctly. "Give me some tips," I begged them. "Well, never get out of your car because that makes us nervous. Keep your hands on the wheel in the ten-to-two-o-clock position, because then we know you are not holding a gun, and we breathe easier. Never contradict us if we say what speed you were doing because that only ticks us off. And the phrase 'Officer, would you consider giving me a break if I tell you why?' is a good ploy to use. If you tell me a good story, give me a laugh, treat me with respect, chances are good I may actually consider it and give you a break—it never hurts to ask. Actually very few people ask."

Now let me repeat the question. If highway patrol pulls you over and threatens to give you a speeding ticket, who has the power—you or highway patrol? Hopefully your answer is that both of you have power, especially you the driver. You now have more information and because you do, you are in a better position to negotiate a ticket. So whether the deal is a billion dollars, a thousand dollars, a ticket, a home, a car, these characters called information, time, power, and the iceberg remain the same.

Key Story to Illustrate the PITI (Power, Information, Time, Iceberg) Model

Tip to the reader. As you read this key story, become active and start asking yourself these two questions:

- What did he do that made this deal successful?

- How can I apply it to my situation?

In January 1983, I arrived in America with the clothes on my back, two suitcases, and $4,700. That was all I possessed. I felt like my fellow countryman Oscar Wilde, who, on being asked at customs in New York if he had anything to declare, famously replied, "Nothing sir, except my genius!" That May, I began work in Silicon Valley for a Fortune 500 Company. I started off as a junior buyer and had an annual budget of $18 million. I must confess to you that I failed my way to success as a negotiator. By that I mean I made many mistakes at the beginning—fortunately for me it was not at the expense of my money, but my company's money. "Don't worry," my mentor told me, "It's okay to make mistakes, but it's not okay to repeat them—you must learn from them and make adjustments." He also gave me this invaluable piece of advice, "Michael, renting is for the birds! You have to buy yourself a home."

Armed with this advice, I set a goal to buy a house within the next six months. I asked a lot of questions from colleagues at work. Where is a good place to buy a home between San Jose (where I worked) and San Francisco where my wife worked? A colleague I admired told me, "Michael, why not try a nice town called San Carlos. It's halfway between San Francisco and San Jose, and it has a great school district." Over the next six weeks, I plagued real estate agents in San Carlos, and each time there was an open house, I was there. They were always talking about "the PITI." One day I said to one of them, "What does PITI mean?" Honestly, I didn't know what it meant. The agent looked at me with pity, saying "Are you serious?" I assured her I was. The heavens opened, and Moses came down from the mountaintop and proclaimed, "Principal, interest, taxes, and insurance." I had arrived at long last at the Promised Land.

I discovered that the median price of a 2-bedroom, 1-bathroom home in San Carlos was about $150,000. Talk about culture shock—I could have bought my whole village in Ireland for $150,000! Eventually we saw a home we liked and my wife said to me, "Michael, why don't you negotiate a good price?" But I thought I didn't have a clue about negotiations. However, when I thought about it further, I said to myself, *Michael, hold it. You were a teacher for many years. In the classroom you were always negotiating with the students.* It was another "aha" moment that we all have—the truth is, we are always negotiating, aren't we? The truth is that many of our conversations are sales situations in which we are trying to sell something—our ideas, our insights, ourselves. Think of the "sale" you had to make to the "prospect" when you proposed marriage or even to just go out on a date!

My Irish Accent Helps

But I digress. Let's get back to the plot. We had seen a home we liked, and I am about to negotiate a deal. I went first of all to the home beside the home I wanted to buy. I knocked at the front door, and a nice elderly woman came out, looking very nervous. (Remember, I had recently left my village in Ireland where nobody locks their doors, so I am wondering why she looks so nervous, as she peeps out the door with the lock still on.) "Pardon me, I am just over from Ireland. I would love to buy the home next door, and I was wondering if I could ask you some questions?" I then discovered that it is a great advantage to have an Irish accent in the West Coast of America. "My great grandfather came from Ireland," I was told, and after a few more minutes of conversation I was ushered into her home. Soon I was enjoying a lovely cup of coffee in her kitchen. "Tell me something about the home next door. What's it like?" "Well I do know the owners have had it on the market for four months, and they are going to Missouri," she told me.

Half an hour later, I made my exit, armed with two key pieces of information—the house had been on the market for four months, and the owners were going to Missouri, where I assumed they would not be paying the enormous mortgage payments they pay in the San Francisco Bay Area. The next evening I parked my car near the home I wanted to buy. It was about 5:30, and once again I went up to the front door and knocked. No reply. I waited until 6:30, and still no one was there. I then decided to wait until 7:00, and, if no one came by then, I had a wasted evening.

About ten minutes to seven, a car pulled up in the driveway. I rushed over, "Are you the owner?" "Yes," the owner replied. "I would love to buy your home. May I have a look around?" Mrs. Holley gave me a tour of her home. When she had finished, I said, "Mrs. Holley, this is a lovely home. You've done a great job on it, and I would love to buy it."

(Now I know some real estate experts would say, "Michael, you fool, never praise a product you are going to buy because if you do, you will pay more for it." I respect the experts but they are not always right. I later discovered that the best salespeople never knock the competition, while the worst do.)

The Power of 80/10/10

We sat down at the kitchen table to discuss the deal. The asking price was $150,000. After about thirty minutes of talking, we got down to action. I said, "The only way I can do this is a sales price of $140,000 through an 80/10/10—that is, $112,000 (80 percent) will come from a lender, $14,000 (10 percent) will come from me as a down payment, and the final 10 percent will come from you in the form of a second mortgage on the home—I am asking you to finance the final 10 percent." To make a long story short, we agreed, and I wrote out a check for $1,000 as a good-faith deposit, which at that time was one half of my net worth! Know what made Julius Caesar one of the greatest generals in history? While he and his armies were invading and conquering some countries in Europe, he always insisted his soldiers burn the bridge behind them. Why? Because he understood human nature, that's why! His soldiers had to go forward or die—going back was not an option. I felt like one of Caesar's soldiers after I signed that check—I had to go forward or lose half my net worth.

I was ecstatic and so was my wife when I rushed back to tell her. "Everything they ever said about America is true," I proclaimed gleefully. "It really is the land of opportunity." The next day, much like Caesar marching into Rome, I triumphantly marched into Bank of America to get my loan of $112,000. I was shocked to hear they would not give me a loan. "Come back in a few years when you have some established credit history, and we will be delighted to consider it," they told me. Furious, I went to Wells Fargo Bank for the loan, only to hear basically the same answer—no. I went to seven banks and heard that terrible word *no*. Frustrated beyond belief, I went to a colleague at work and said, "I am having a hell of a time getting a loan from these banks—what should I do?" She was a real estate agent part-time, and I kidded her about being a buyer by day, real estate agent by night. "Oh Michael, I'm glad you asked. Don't go near banks—you are only wasting your time. You see, banks have all kinds of guidelines to follow, Fannie Mae guidelines, Freddie Mac guidelines, and the government monitors them. You're not long in the country—you have no credit history. You'll never get a loan this year from them. You are going to have to go to a mortgage company—they are not banks, but they do make in-house loans. That's the good news. The bad news is you will have to pay more for the loan, in the form of higher fees and a higher interest rate, but if you want a loan this year, that's the price you are going to have to pay."

I started calling some mortgage companies in San Francisco, with two questions, "Who is the most senior vice president and is he/she humane?" I figured I needed all the help I could get at this stage. Eventually I got a name to match my description. I wrote a nice short letter marked *Personal and Confidential*:

Dear Mr. Vice-President. My name is Michael Geraghty and I would really appreciate it if I could meet you for no more than thirty minutes to discuss my loan request of $112,000.

The following week I received a letter from the vice president, advising me to be in his office in San Francisco the following Wednesday at 3:00 PM.

Dress for Success

On Wednesday, I dressed very carefully for this important interview. First of all, I donned my Calvin Klein blue jacket. Let me explain. That January I had arrived at San Francisco Airport in what I thought was a "cool" suit. I had bought it in a store in Ireland, and I got off the plane feeling I looked like a million dollars in my suit. My fiancé met me, and after a big hug, said, "Michael, where did you get that suit? It's awful. It has to go." A few days later she dragged me down to Saks 5th Avenue in San Francisco, where she bought me a $300 Calvin Klein jacket. I smiled as I put on my jacket over my smart gray pants, power tie, and power shirt. I was looking very powerful! I looked at myself in the mirror and was impressed with what I saw: "You're looking good, Michael. This interview will go very well for you. You've been successful in Ireland, and you will be successful in America." Armed with these affirmations and my brand-new briefcase, I drove to the mortgage company to meet the vice president.

"Good afternoon, Mr. Geraghty, please be seated. Can I get you some coffee?" "No thanks, your time is precious, so let's get down to business." "Where does your accent come from?" "I'm Irish." "Oh, may I ask how long you are in the country?" As confidently as I could, I said, "Seven months." The smile evaporated from the face of the vice president as this news sank in. "I see. May I also ask how long you are in your present job?" Again, mustering my confidence, I said, "Seven weeks." The vice president went quiet. "Let me understand this correctly—you are in the country seven months and in your job seven weeks, and you want me to loan you $112,000. Is that correct?" "Yes." "Mr. Geraghty, I respect your time, and my time is also precious. I want you to think about this—you are in the country seven months, in your job seven weeks, so why should I loan you $112,000?"

Notice (1) we are in the first quarter of the game, and I am having an absolutely terrible first quarter. Two touchdowns have been scored against me, and I haven't had the ball in my hands yet. An important point I want to make to you is this—negotiation is a four-quarter game. You can have a terrible first quarter and still come out fine in the fourth quarter. Novice negotiators are inclined to panic, if they get off to a bad start. Remember Michael Jordan—everybody remembers him in the fourth quarter when he got hot—few recall the first quarter when he was cold and missed many shots. I have seen great negotiators having a poor first half. Then they make the adjustments and come out roaring for the second half. Notice (2) the vice president is looking at the top of the iceberg only and alarm bells are ringing. My job as a negotiator is to get him down under the surface to see another side of the problem and hopefully improve my chances of success.

Testimonials Are Great

I calmly told the vice president why he should loan me $112,000. "Mr. Vice President, the reason my present net worth is not big is that I was a teacher for many years in Ireland. If you want to make money I suggest you never become a teacher." The vice president smiled. "Furthermore, my wife has excellent credit, and here is a testimonial from my company—it's a Fortune 500 Company in Silicon Valley." I picked up my briefcase and took out the testimonial, which stated: "To whom it may concern. This is to certify that Michael Geraghty is working in Procurement and has an extremely bright future in our Fortune 500 Company." It was signed by a "Mr. P. Delaney, manager of procurement." To make a long story short, after a disastrous first quarter, I was still in the office of the vice president, and he hadn't thrown me out. After some more questions and answers he looked at me strangely and said this: "Mr. Geraghty, I regard you as an interesting challenge. In fact you remind me of my great-grandfather who left Russia in 1897 and never got a break when he came to America. I don't want to raise your hopes unduly because the chance of you getting this loan is less than 50/50. I want to give more consideration to your loan application. I have all the information I need and will call you next week with my decision. However, I do want to make it clear again that my decision to say yes is less than 50/50." I thanked him for his time and left the office.

Each time the phone rang the following week, I was hoping it would be the vice president with some news, hopefully good news. No call came that week and I was beginning to lose hope. Tuesday of the following week the phone rang—"Is that you, Mr. Geraghty, this is the vice president. I have good news for you. I was able to persuade them to approve the loan. Best of luck to you." I was now 80 percent of the way up the financial mountain.

Just as my friend at work had warned me, this loan was going to cost me more money in points and fees. When all the dust had settled, the bottom line on my 10 percent down payment came to $19,200. I had $2,000 to my name at this point. My fiancé had $7,000, so I was short $11,000. Remember, I am a country boy, born and reared in a village in Ireland. Country boys are interdependent, and all that means is that "we" is so much stronger than "I." I am so much stronger with others than I am alone. I got on the phone to my two brothers-in-law and made this deal: "Between the two of you, could you loan me $11,000 for three years at 10 percent interest only, with a balloon payment of $11,000 due in three years?" Within three days they wired me the money, and in September 1983, eight months after arriving in America with $5,000, we moved into our tiny home in San Carlos, California.

See how deals are done? In the next chapter, we will go back over this deal, pick out some things I did that worked for me, and then explore together how those same things will work for you in your situation.

Key Points

- Negotiation is a drama with four characters—power, information, time, and iceberg. Get to know these characters intimately because when you do, you will become a master negotiator. This book will make you very familiar with each one of them.

- Studies reveal that many negotiators always think the other side has more power than they do. You may need to change your paradigm.

- Whether the deal is a billion dollars or a hundred dollars, these four characters remain the same.

- Negotiation is a four-quarter game.

- Negotiation is the use of power, information, time, and rapport (iceberg) to get what you want and also to help other people get what they want.

3

Power

Think again about the key story I told you about buying my first home. I hope that during it you were asking yourself a few questions:

- How did he put that deal together?

- What skills did he use?

- What lessons can I learn from what he did?

In my workshops, I usually break people into groups of three, and ask them to come up with their answers to the above questions. Here are seven powers that were used in the story:

- Power of Attitude

- Power of Goals

- Power of Perseverance

- Power of Preparation

- Power of Questions

- Power of Positive Expectations

- Power of Identification

Power of Attitude

Is attitude important? I would have to say it is #1 in life. I brought a certain attitude into that interview with the vice president. I was determined not to go in like a beggar asking for mercy. Loan officers are not in the business of charity—they are in the business of making hard decisions on loans. I did not feel at all like a beggar in an unequal relationship. Here is one of my favorite mantras:

* *What happens to you is not half as important as how you* **react** *to what happens to you.*

In other words, you get what you expect. The following story is about some pioneers in covered wagons who crossed into the new Oregon territory. They stopped to rest at a small settlement and the wagon master spoke to an old man sunning himself in front of the general store. "Say, old-timer, what kind of people have settled out here?" "What kind of people were they where you came from?" asked the old man. "Well, they were mean, full of mischief, and small-minded. That's why we left," said the wagon master.

"Sorry to say, young feller, but that's the kind of folks you'll find out here," replied the old man.

Later in the week, another team of wagons pulled into town for supplies. This wagon master also stopped in front of the general store and saw the same old man sunning himself on the steps. "Say, old-timer, what kind of people have settled out here?"

"What kind of people were they where you came from?" asked the old man again. "The people we left behind were kind, decent people, and they were generous. When we left them, they gave us supplies and helped us load our wagons. We all miss them very much, sighed the wagon master."

"Well, my friend, you've come to the right place because those are the kind of people you're going to find out here," replied the old man with a kindly smile.

What is the moral of this story? You get what you expect. Bring an attitude like this to your own life, and all your negotiations and your chances of success are dramatically improved.

Here's a mantra for you to always remember:

* Excellent attitude produces excellent results.

* Good attitude produces good results.

- Poor attitude produces poor results.

I have these three lines embedded in my memory, whenever I negotiate. It is a universal law. It doesn't matter if you're rich or poor, black or white, Republican or Democrat, man or woman, Christian or Muslim. It is, and always will be, one of the greatest laws of life.

Are You a Leader or a Follower?

Throughout their lives many people are "taught" to be followers. As children, teachers "taught" them. Then society "molded" them into adults, which naturally allowed politicians to "lead" them, bosses to "manage" them, and religious leaders to "guide" them. Adults are meant to guide themselves, but how many do? A lot of people we know are content to be regulated and manipulated, rather than to make their own rules and lead their own lives. So the question is very important—are you a leader or a follower?

Let me put this question to you. Assume you are a Catholic and that the Pope is someone you respect very much. You are in a dilemma. Your personal conscience is telling you to do something, but your Pope is telling you not to do it. What should you do? If you say, "I will do what the Pope says," you are outer-directed (you depend on others to make up your mind.) If you said, "I respect and admire the Pope, but I must follow my conscience despite what the Pope says," you are inner-directed (you depend on yourself and trust your instincts when it comes to making decisions.) What has all this got to do with negotiation? All the surveys tell us that the best negotiators are inner-directed.

To be an effective negotiator, your attitude is the most important ingredient. To be a skilled negotiator, you need a leader's attitude. You can decide for yourself what you want, and how to go after it. Be a leader. It is amazing how this attitude will transform your life.

Power of Goals

In the story I had a very simple goal—to buy a house. Goals are very important aren't they? Most people I ask say, "Yes, of course, goals are very important." Well if they are so important, why is it that only 3 percent of Americans have written goals? Let me say something about the power of written goals. Many people say it's okay once you have goals, but there's no need to have them in writing. Really? Let me give you this example. Two people are equally talented. One says,

"Someday I'll have the salary I deserve."
"Someday my boss will appreciate the job I am doing."
"Someday I'll be happy and successful."

The other says,

"Okay, today I am earning $50,000. Within the next twenty-four months I will be earning $75,000 and this is how I am going to do it, quarter-by-quarter, month-by-month, week-by-week. Here are my written weekly goals to achieve my objective." Who do you think has the better chance of making it? The answer is obvious isn't it? The person with written goals always has a huge advantage.

Many people live on the very popular island called "Someday I'll…" We hear it all around us:

"Someday I'll have enough money to retire."
"Someday I'll be rich and successful."
"Someday I'll get what I deserve."

I wish them well, but vague goals like that are a hill of beans. Ultimately they get you nowhere. If you don't know where you are going, chances are good you are not going to get there.

The same applies to negotiation. I am always amazed at the number of people who go into negotiations with no written goals. My mentor insisted I always have negotiation goals in writing. Ever since, whenever I do business I always have three written goals:

1. What I would love to get out of this negotiation.

2. What I would like to get out of this negotiation.

3. If it's below a certain price (depending if I am a seller), I'm passing on the deal.

Let's say I am thinking of selling my home. Fair market value is $300,000. I would love to get $310,000. I would like to get $290,000. But if the buyers offer less than $275,000 I am not going to waste my time discussing it—I will pass on the deal. You'd be surprised at how much this simple little exercise will help you, whenever you do business.

Let's say you are the buyer interested in buying the home above. As the buyer you have your goals in writing. I would love to get it for $260,000. I would like to get it for $275,000. If it gets to $290,000 I am going to pass on the deal. Once again, you'd be surprised at how helpful this is when you are the buyer. If you want to get it for $260,000, you'd better start with a low offer of $240,000.

The Art of Compromise

Remember, the buyer always wants the lowest possible price. The seller always wants the highest possible price. Negotiation is the game that takes place as they try to persuade each other. The buyer hopes the seller will come down in price. The seller hopes the buyer will come up in price. It is a chess game with different buyer moves and different seller moves. Welcome to the wonderful chess game of negotiation.

Peak performers have many things in common. One of them is written goals. The famous sales trainer Tom Hopkins, a peak performer himself, once said this: "Goals are the fuel in the furnace of achievement." If you want to achieve great success in negotiations, remember that written goals are the price you have to pay. It's as simple as that. However, if you don't have written goals in life, you are probably not going to have them in negotiation. I highly recommend a great book on the power of goals called *How to Get Control of Your Time and Your Life* by Alan Lakein, a time management expert. I have used it myself and it has been of enormous help. You will find it very easy reading, with some great simple exercises on how to set goals.

- Why do so many people not have written goals?

- You may have to do a paradigm shift.

Power of Perseverance

When you enter the world of negotiation, you must get used to hearing the word no.

If you recall the story I told you about getting my loan, I heard an awful lot of no's, didn't I? I went to seven banks and I was turned down by all seven. One thing I have always noticed about world-class negotiators—they don't get too depressed when they hear a lot of no's. In fact for a good negotiator, no does not mean no! I am serious. For many people, no means no. A refusal is a refusal. If a person says no, they figure the person is serious. Not so with great negotiators. No does not mean no—it just means maybe. Let me explain. The prospect has turned the product down by saying "No, I am not interested in your product." The great negotiators say to themselves, *Okay, I haven't made the sale yet—I will have to think of another way of selling it better to this prospect.*

I was recently reading a fascinating study on top salespeople. I discovered that the top 10 percent of salespeople working in high-tech earn more than the bottom 90 percent combined. Astounding, isn't it? The 80/20 Pareto rule is a very interesting one. For example, in real estate offices this is a well-known secret:

• 20 percent of the agents bring in 80 percent of the money.

• 80 percent of the agents bring in 20 percent of the money.

The study concerned this magical 10 percent who earn the same as the other 90 percent combined. People wanted to get inside the heads of these top 10 percent. They wanted to find out the secret of their success—why they performed as they did, and could their skills be transferred to some of the other salespeople in the bottom 90 percent. So they went to the top 10 percent and asked them this question: Assuming you had qualified the prospect,

"How many times must a prospect say no before you would pass on the deal?"

They were shocked to hear the answer. "We do not understand the question." "Well, let's rephrase it, and say you are trying to persuade the prospect to buy your product and the prospect turns you down. The prospect rejects your product. How many times would it take for you to experience this rejection, before you would pass on the deal?" The top 10 percent said, "Sorry, we still don't understand the question."

So they went to the bottom 90 percent, who had no problem with the question. Many of them were gone after the first no. All of them were gone after the third no. The 90 percent did not understand the key secret of the top 10 percent, which is—if you "play the numbers game" with all your prospects, if you don't take no for an answer, if you persist, if you keep on going, the numbers will eventually work out in your favor. The top 10 percent understood that you have to play the numbers. They understood how many times you must make the attempt to sell before the numbers work out to your advantage. The answer is five and a half attempts. For example, you may go to the first prospect who says yes—great, but understand that you may go to ten prospects, all of whom say no, but the eleventh prospect says yes. If you play the numbers, and don't get discouraged by no's, the numbers will work for you, as long as you are ready to accept a lot of no's.

Sometimes a Bad Memory is a Good Thing

When you enter the world of negotiation, you must get used to hearing the word no. I heard John Madden, the great NFL analyst and broadcaster, talk about a key skill desperately needed by all great cornerbacks. "They must have a lousy memory," he said. "They have just been burned for a touchdown, and immediately they have to forget what just happened, and get ready for the next play." Great negotiators have the same skill—they have just been burned by a no. They must forget they heard no, and concentrate on persuading the prospect to go for the product. Notice how kids have this skill. No does not mean no to a kid—it just means "maybe." The kid says silently, *Maybe if I try a tantrum, Dad will change the* no *into a* maybe. The next time you are tempted to say, "Which part of the no do you not understand, is it the *n* part or the *o* part?" just remember kids do what kids do instinctively because it works! It works for kids and it will work for you in negotiation too.

I have often heard the following whenever I am selling my training programs to decision makers:

"I'm really not interested."
"Business is terrible right now."
"I am very happy with my present provider."
"Let me think about it and I'll get back to you."

See what I mean about the need for persistence when you negotiate? Persistence is a terrific skill in life—and in negotiation.

The Power of Preparation

* Fail to plan, and you plan to fail.

Here are my three rules for preparation:

1. Always do your homework.

2. Always do your homework.

3. Always do your homework.

World-class negotiators have many things in common. One of the major things I have observed about them is their utter dedication to preparation.

- *What water is to a garden, homework is to negotiation.*

When I was first trained as a negotiator in Silicon Valley, my mentor told me, "Michael, anytime you are negotiating a deal worth more than half a million dollars, I want you to think about the magic 8:1 formula—do at least eight hours of preparation, for each hour of negotiation. I thought I was doing well until I first started negotiating in Japan with Fujitsu Corporation, the #2 computer-maker in the world, with 150,000 employees and $80 billion in revenues. One night I was out drinking with some Japanese negotiators. The subject got around to the importance of preparation in business. I proudly told them I used the 8:1 ratio, expecting them to be shocked and awed. Turns out I was the one who was shocked and awed—"Geraghty-san" (they put—*san* at the end of your last name when they are getting comfortable with you), "our ratio is 17:1." The Japanese are fanatics about details, and that includes negotiation. For those of you who have to do business with the Japanese, you will now understand why they are always asking questions. Just when you think you have answered every question, they have some more. Relax! The Japanese are just doing their 17:1 ratio.

I prepared very carefully for the interview with the vice president. Even though I knew very little about negotiation, I knew a lot about the importance of preparation, from my sporting days. I had played rugby for many years, and any rugby player will tell you that all the hours of preparation you do *before* you run on to the playing field are vital—all those hours when you sweat during rigorous training, all the mental preparation you do as you size up your opponent ahead of the game, even the light meal you take before the game—all will help you win the game. It was in Japan one evening that a Japanese quoted for me the famous quote from *The Art of War* by Sun Tzu:

"All battles are won **before** they are fought."

While I was preparing for the interview I asked myself this question, *what are some questions he may ask?* The more I thought about it, and the more I prepared, I began to realize that I had better have some satisfactory explanation for two key questions he was likely to ask:

- "How long are you in the country?"

- "How long are you in your present job?"

Ted Kennedy

Michael, I said to myself, *These are killer questions, especially the one about the job. How are you going to get around it? And don't do a Ted Kennedy on it!* Let me explain. In the summer of 1980 I was in America when Ted Kennedy was running for president. One evening I was channel surfing when all of a sudden I saw Ted being interviewed by Roger Mudd. In the middle of the interview, Mudd said, "Senator Kennedy, why do you want to be president?" Over the next few minutes, I could not believe what I was actually looking at—Ted stumbled and stuttered, scratching his head, and it became obvious to me he was not prepared for the question. He did not give a satisfying answer. I said to myself, *Ted, if you don't know why you want to be president, why should anyone go to the bother of voting for you?* Turned out that Ted did not get to be president, and I never forgot his stumbling performance that evening.

I decided then that I had better get a testimonial from my boss, as a way of taking the sting out of my seven weeks on the job. In fact as I was mentally rehearsing the interview, I turned myself down for the loan because I was too risky! I later discovered that the best defense attorneys in America first figure out what the prosecutors are likely to do with their case *before* they ever start on their defense.

When the vice president asked me why he should loan me $112,000, I knew this was not the time to wing it. I was prepared for the question ahead of time, and because I was prepared, I was confident of being able to handle it.

The next time you buy a car, the next time you sell a home, the next time you do a job interview, or sell an idea at work, remember the power of preparation.

- What water is to a garden, homework is to negotiation.

- All battles are won *before* they are fought.

- Fail to plan, and you plan to fail.

The Power of Asking Questions

Observe in the story the number of questions I asked:

> "Can you tell me anything about the house next door?"
> "Where can I find a home between San Francisco and San Jose?"
> "Hey boss, can you give me a testimonial?"
> "Seven banks have turned me down, so where can I get a loan?"

The story is really a series of questions. I have noticed that great negotiators ask lots of questions—not any kind of questions, but questions that will give them key pieces of information so they can do the deal and be successful.

I have a question for you. You watch *60 Minutes* or *20/20* and you see great interviewers asking questions. Who has more power during the interviews—they who ask the questions, or they who answer them? I believe it is they who ask the questions. The same goes whenever you do business. After fifteen years of observing salespeople in Silicon Valley, I have discovered that the best of them spend a lot of time asking the right kind of questions.

Think about it: if you are talking, you are not learning. If you are talking, you don't have time to pay too much attention to the prospect. However, if you are asking questions and listening carefully, what do you think is happening inside the head of your prospect? I do workshops for buyers all over America. I often ask them their pet peeve about salespeople. You probably guessed it already—salespeople talk too much. Salespeople don't listen enough.

Socrates

Socrates has given his name to one of the most important ideas in education—if you ask the students the right questions, their education will be improved and they learn far more effectively. It is called the Socratic method. It works in education, it works in business, and it is especially powerful in negotiations.

One of the most interesting people I have ever met was Bernhard Haring. What Tigers Woods is to golf, what Barbara Walters is to interviewers, what

Peter Drucker is to consultants, Bernhard Haring is to moral theologians—he is regarded as the greatest moral theologian of the twentieth century. He was in Dublin, Ireland, where I heard him speak on prayer. The auditorium was packed with people, ready to listen to the great theologian speak. He did a very strange thing. "I am not going to lecture to you today. I want to break you into groups of four, and I have this question for you to discuss—where do you experience God? And I do not want to hear about church, I want to hear about your life." Over the next two and a half hours, I learned more about prayer from that question than I could ever learn from someone just lecturing about it. My group of four talked about personal experiences of God in their lives. See what I mean by smart use of the Socratic method?

Salespeople have discovered the same. They have discovered that if they ask the right questions of the prospect, the sale becomes easier. The top salespeople now listen 70 percent of the time and the only way they can do this is to ask questions. You do the same and see what happens:

"May I ask you how did you decide on the price?"
"Can you tell me something about your requirements?"
"If there were one key reason for you to buy my product, what would it be?"
"What would make you happy?"
"How can we get this deal back on track?"
"Who are the key decision makers in this major account?"
"Would you consider doing me a favor?"

Socrates was right. The Bible was right—"Ask and you shall receive."

Power of Positive Expectations

"If you think you can or if you think you can't, you're right."—Henry Ford

Great negotiators always expect to do very well whenever they negotiate. You should do the same. Great athletes do it—so should you. I went into the interview with the vice president expecting to do well, based on my past experiences of dealing with decision makers.

Consider this true story. A fascinating experiment was carried out in a large school district in San Francisco. At the beginning of the school year, three teachers were asked to step into the principal's office. They had to sign confidentiality agreements first. Then the principal said, "We are going to do a top secret project this school year. Do not breathe a word of this to anybody—not your spouse, not your mentor, not your best friend. It has been determined that you three are the top three teachers in this school. We are going to give each of you the top students for your classes. They are "the cream of the crop." Do not change your teaching style. Do everything as you have done before. This is very important. Do not change anything in your teaching style. At the end of each semester, we will compare how your three classes are doing, and compare them with the other classes."

Productivity Improvement of 21 Percent

Christmas came and, when the grades were compared, it was discovered that the top three classes with the top three teachers had grades that exceeded the others by 21 percent. Easter came, and they were ahead by 19 percent. When summer came, they were ahead by 23 percent. So, over the course of the school year, the average improvement was 21 percent.

At the end of school year, the principal brought in the three teachers. "Congratulations," she said, "this project has exceeded all our expectations. There has been an average 21 percent improvement in performance within your classes. These results really have been splendid." The teachers smiled and said, "Thank you, but you really should not be too surprised, as we are the three best teachers in the school." The principal looked uncomfortable. "Actually," she said, "I brought you in to explain that we took your names and placed them in a drum with all the other teacher names—your three names came out at random." It was the teacher's turn to be surprised. "Well, we may not be the top three teachers, but you did give us the top students, and that is what made the huge difference of an increased 21 percent improvement in performance." Now the principal was looking even more uncomfortable. "I apologize," she said, "I did not mean to be devious at the beginning of the school year. This has been a special project authorized by the superintendent of schools, and I too had to sign a confidentiality agreement. I did not give you the top students, though I told you I did. Once again, I placed all the student names in a drum and picked them out at random."

I have a question for you—given what you now know about the above story, how can you explain a 21 percent productivity improvement? It is called the Law of Positive Expectations. If you treat students like they're bright and smart, students pick up on that and try to prove you right. On the contrary, if you treat them like they're not bright and smart, students pick up on that as well.

- If a child learns to live with criticism, the child will criticize.

- If a child learns to live with hatred, the child will hate.

- If a child learns to live in an atmosphere of positive expectations, the child will thrive.

Some people expect the best and some people expect the worst.

I always go into negotiations expecting the best. I expect to do well. I expect that the people across the table are ethical and good. Am I sometimes horribly disappointed? You better believe I am. But I always expect the best. Why? Because that is what I have seen very successful people do. So I don't fight it intellectually. If it works for them, that's enough for me. So I went into my interview with the vice president expecting to do well. Try it and see for yourself.

The Power of Identification

During the interview, I managed to identify myself with the vice president. He told me so himself: "You remind me of my great-grandfather from Russia." You will maximize your negotiating ability if you get others to identify with you. Think about these questions:

- Why do you prefer one store to another?

- Why do you take your car to the same service station?

- Why use one bank instead of another?

- In your business world, why do you deal with one company and not another?

The answer is surprisingly simple—the power of identification is at work.

I did a lot of business with Fujitsu Corporation of Japan. It was like dealing with the U.S. federal government—absolutely huge. How did this huge company identify with me? A few individuals within Fujitsu established a personal relationship with me. I don't think of 150,000 people—I think of Suzuki-san and

Tanaka-san and a few others. Smart salespeople, who work for huge corporations like IBM, understand this. They make the huge corporation personal.

Twice, the IRS decided they wanted to audit me for aggressive deductions in real estate. Now that sounds very intimidating, doesn't it? I still have the "dreaded" notice in my office—"The IRS versus Michael F. Geraghty." I did not think of the whole IRS when I went in to that audit—I thought of the one IRS person who was going to interview me. If I could somehow identify with that person, it would be smart. I tried to position myself as an honest taxpayer and to help me understand if I made any mistakes. It worked, and I got out of those two interviews with a mild slap on the wrist and was asked to only pay a few hundred dollars.

The power of identification also works in reverse. You give a bad impression, and by association, your company's name and reputation suffer. We all know people who may be right but are obnoxious—that can kill a negotiation. Therefore, use and beware of the power of identification. The key rule here is, personalize, personalize, and personalize.

Key Points

- Here are just a few of your powers—the power of attitude, goals, perseverance, preparation, questions, positive expectations, and identification.

- Excellent attitude produces excellent results, good attitude produces good results, and poor attitude produces poor results. This is a universal law.

- All the surveys tell us that the best negotiators are inner-directed.

- Only 3 percent of Americans have written goals. The negotiator with written goals always has a huge advantage.

- The buyer always wants the lowest price, and the seller always wants the highest price. Negotiation is the game that takes place as they try to persuade each other.

- When you enter the world of negotiation, get used to hearing the word no.

- The top 10 percent of salespeople earn the same as the other 90 percent combined.

- The top salespeople now listen 70 percent of the time.

- Great negotiators always expect to do very well when they negotiate.

- You will maximize your negotiating ability if you get others to identify with you.

4

Information

There is a direct ratio between information and leverage. The negotiator who has the most leverage is usually the one with the best information.

- *The more you know about your own product...*

- *The more you know about your own company...*

- *The more you know about your competition...*

- *The more you know about the buyer/seller...*

- *The more you know about their organization...*

...the stronger your position is whenever you negotiate.

Some years ago, a salesperson told me this story. "I was in a new negotiation with a long-time customer. The buyer was doing her buyer thing: 'The price is too high; the competition is fierce; they had some late shipments; and their failure rate was higher than expected.' She didn't know that a week earlier one of my support people had been talking to an end user at her company, who said, 'Are we glad your company is providing these! There've been some flaws and one of them breaks now and then, but that's nothing compared to the last outfit they bought these from. Their service was lousy, and they didn't even return our phone calls.'" Guess who has the leverage in this negotiation?

As a buyer, I cringe when I hear the above story. Those kinds of comments are said in every industry. Therefore, if you are a seller, isn't it to your advantage to know how the buyer's engineers or end users feel about your product? That is why top salespeople spend a lot of time and energy talking to the people in the trenches, the people who use their products. They ask questions, looking for information that will give them leverage.

When I was trying to buy my first home, I got some great information by just asking questions from the neighbors:

"Can you tell me something about the seller?"
"How long has the house been for sale?"
"Why is the seller selling?"

One half-hour of asking questions saved me a lot of money and it will do the very same for you.

The Leak Information Model

Imagine information as another drama in which there are four main characters again. The character names are called:

- **L**everage

- **E**xpertise

- **A**sk unusual questions

- **K**ey issues

Get an understanding of how these characters play their roles, and you will have the keys to the kingdom. All the surveys prove that those who do best in any negotiation are those who have the best information.

Leverage: Little pieces of Key Information Work Wonders

Whenever I talk to executives in Silicon Valley, I notice that many of them use certain words. I often hear them talk about the importance of execution. I'm not talking about the death penalty here—simply the execution of the corporate plan. Another word they love is the word *leverage*. Leverage means making a little do a lot. Let's explore how you can make a little do a lot.

Consider physical leverage. When I bought my first rental house, it needed some loving tender care. I decided to paint it and immediately fell in love with physical leverage. By that I mean I could paint 80 percent of it in 20 percent of the time. I fell passionately in love with big long paint rollers. I was most impressed with how fast they could paint. *This is great*, I smugly said to myself, *I'll have this paint job done in no time at all.* Later, I discovered that is the best part of painting—the worst part, of course, is the details that take 80 percent of your time—those small tiny brushes for the corners and all the other detail work that must be done. Ever since, I have had a love-hate relationship with paint rollers and small brushes.

Consider time leverage. Do you know people who can do more in four hours than others in two days? Of course you do—we all know them. They are amazing aren't they? Tom Hopkins, the great sales motivational speaker, was once asked the secret of how he can get so much done so quickly. He said, "My mentor gave me this piece of advice which I never forgot: 'Tom, promise me that the last thing you will do each evening is this—write down in order of importance, the six most important things you have to do tomorrow.' That is my secret. I know of no better way to keep myself focused. It works for me, and it will work for you." Tom can do more in four hours than most will do in four days because he is goal-oriented, he is crystal clear, and he is focused. Most of us are not that way. Most start off their day not sure about their goals for the day. Consequently, they waste a lot of time "getting ready to get ready."

Information Leverage

Now I come to the main point of this exercise: information leverage. If you were to ask me what are the top two things world-class negotiators do, one of them would be this—they leverage information. They make little pieces of key information work wonders. When I first came to America in 1983, I started hearing a lot about Lee Iacocca—CEO of Ford Motor Company. He was fired from Ford and then became CEO of Chrysler Corporation. For a time it looked like he had jumped out of the frying pan into the fire because Chrysler was almost going into bankruptcy.

Iacocca was always a man of action. In his hour of need, he confidently went to see his Republican friends in Congress and asked them for a $1 billion loan to prevent Chrysler from declaring bankruptcy. His Republican friends said, "Lee, we love you and we are so grateful for all your help and financial support over the years, but we have to tell you, giving a $1 billion loan in this instance goes against all our Republican principles. Sorry, we can't do it."

Did that stop Iacocca in his tracks? Of course it didn't. Remember what I said about persistence. Remember what I said about great negotiators—they don't hear no when it is said to them? The old saying is correct: "When the going gets tough, the tough get going." Iacocca said to himself, *Who the hell in Washington can help me*? He asked a few movers and shakers in Washington, and one of them said, "Lee, why don't you see Tip O'Neill, the speaker of the house—he's about ·the only who can advise you."

"Tip," said Iacocca, "I'm in a real jam and I need your help." "What's the problem, Lee?" "I've just seen some Republican friends because I am looking for a $1 billion loan from the federal government. They tell me they can't help me. I've asked a few movers and shakers and doers in Washington and they tell me to see you. Here I am." "Let's meet tomorrow for breakfast," said O'Neill, "and I'll see what can be done."

Over breakfast, O'Neill said, "Lee, you must understand that all politics is local. You have to make your problem local for your Republican friends in Congress. The only way to persuade them to loan you a billion dollars is to bring to their attention the ripple effects of a Chrysler bankruptcy on their local Republican districts. That means the dealerships go—no local tax revenues. Workers have to go; local tax revenues are again affected. You have to get your Chrysler bean counters working overtime and send the financials to your Republican friends. I guarantee you that will get their attention."

The minute O'Neill said that, Iacocca knew exactly what he had to do. He called in his chief financial officer, gave the orders, and within seventy-two hours, each Republican member of congress had the local effects of a Chrysler bankruptcy. You'll never guess what happened. That's how Iacocca got his loan. Note the challenge and how he got it. His challenge was to persuade hard-nosed politicians to do something they didn't want to do. He asked a key question—who can help me pull this off? He got the answer and executed the plan superbly.

How Can You Leverage Information?

Ever notice how experts influence people? I am not talking about being an expert in astrophysics. My German brother-in-law, Gerhard, is an expert on Volkswagens because for many years that was his profession. When his friends had any problem with their cars, they turned to him for advice because he was the car expert. My brother Patrick is a fabulous storyteller, and people are always asking him to tell a story. Why? Because he is an expert at what he does. My mother-in-law, Bonnie, is a fantastic cook. You will not be surprised when I tell you she is often asked for advice on cooking.

Corporate America loves experts, and pays dearly for their expertise. This may surprise you—have you ever considered becoming an information expert in a small area? Most people never have. Here is a tip I have been giving for ten years, and let me share it now with you. Decide to become an information expert in a small area and see what happens to you. This idea intimidates most people—"Me an expert, that's a laugh!" I am totally serious. To make it less intimidating, let's break it down like this—spend one hour a day in becoming an expert, and within three to five years you will be an expert. I call this the hour of power. Set aside one hour each day to educate yourself.

The Hour of Power

Let me explain. When I first came to America, I knew absolutely nothing about real estate. At a seminar in San Francisco in 1984, I was introduced to this idea of the hour of power and becoming an information expert in a small area. I decided to become an information expert in real estate. I set a goal of one hour each work-day—five hours a week, twenty-three hours a month. I went to the local library and borrowed books on real estate. I started going to workshops on real estate. I attended real estate courses on real estate principles, real estate law, and real estate finance techniques.

While I was doing this, I noticed some things about myself that may help you. It took me a few months to meet my goal of one hour each business day. I started measuring my time carefully—each time I did anything on real estate, I made a note—ten minutes here, forty minutes here, and two hours there. Some months I did only ten hours, so I had to have a serious talk with myself. Slowly but surely I started hitting my goal. What I am trying to tell you here is this—don't be discouraged if you don't achieve your goal immediately. Start measuring your time spent, and be patient.

I noticed something else—I didn't see any difference the first six or seven months I was doing this, and you won't either. Again don't be discouraged. If you continue to do it for twelve, eighteen, or twenty-four months, not only will you begin to notice a difference, other people will too. I started buying properties and applying what I was learning to actually buying real estate. Slowly but surely, like waves breaking on the seashore, I became an information expert in a small area.

In a nutshell, here is your strategy template:

- Decide to become an information expert in a small area.

- Ask a few key people you respect for guidance in the area you want to be an expert in.

- Measure your time.

- Reward yourself occasionally for goals achieved along the way.

- Enjoy the learning journey.

For the past ten years, I have been giving this tip about the hour of power. I wish I could share with you some of the e-mails and phone calls I have received from people who took this idea and ran with it. Within a three-to-five-to-seven-year stretch, some of them doubled, tripled, and quadrupled their income. The secret is to find an idea or an area that you have some passion in. Commit yourself to the hour of power and go do it.

I have always loved this quote:

"Blessed are those who dream dreams and are willing to pay the price to make them come true."

Intellectual Capital

I was fascinated when I first started reading the history of the San Francisco Bay Area and the role that gold played in its rapid expansion. In the 1840s, hard to believe, San Francisco was just a small town. Then gold was discovered, the population exploded, and San Francisco was never the same. What happened? Gold happened. Physical gold revolutionized the whole area. That was the nineteenth century. In the twenty-first century, the new gold is not physical. The new gold is intellectual. The new gold is intellectual capital, and the new entrepreneurs of this century are riding the intellectual capital wave. You can too, so what is stopping you, except perhaps yourself?

Make Your Car a Mobile Classroom

I gave this tip recently in Silicon Valley, and I could see one gentleman rolling up his eyes. "What's up?" I said. "Well the idea is great, but my problem is I already have a sixty-five-hour week, not counting a horrendous commute. Sorry, I need to do another hour a day like I need a broken leg!" I suggested this idea to him. "I understand how you feel. That is tough. However, have you ever thought of your car as a university on wheels? Have you ever thought of your car as a mobile classroom?" "No I haven't. What exactly do you mean?" "Well, I know some top salespeople who are totally committed to lifelong education. Like you, they work hard, but they educate themselves while they are driving. They tell me you can become one of the best-educated people in America by listening to tapes or CDs while you drive. That is how they do their hour a day and so can you."

Another objection I heard is this one: "Great—I love this idea of the hour of power, but I don't have the money. I can just about make the rent each month. I can't afford these tapes and books and videos and CDs." My reply was this: "Did you know you can still do all this without spending a dime? That's right—by not spending a dime. The American library system is one of the jewels of the world, courtesy of people like Andrew Carnegie. Start having an affair with your local library. There you can borrow free books, videos, CDs, and tapes on all kinds of subjects that interest you." What excuse do you have? If you think about the above objections, they may be excuses not to act. The old saying is true: "Obstacles are what you see when you take your eye off the goal."

Becoming an Expert

In 1996, I decided to leave my company and well-paid job and start my own training and consulting business. I asked a lot of questions of people I respected. One of the best pieces of advice I got was this: "Michael, become an expert in one area that you have credibility in. Many speakers speak on all kinds of subjects—they are jack-of-all-trades but masters-of-none. Corporate America pays dearly for experts in their field." I thought about this and asked myself this important question: *What do you have credibility in?* Gradually the word *negotiation* sprung to mind. *Michael, you did a lot of investing in real estate, and you did an awful lot of negotiating with suppliers all over the world, when you worked in Silicon Valley. Why don't you use the hour of power to get up to speed on negotiation?* I did and it has meant a huge increase in the fees I charge because I am perceived to be an expert in a small area that is important to some people.

Then I asked this question: *Who would want to hear what I have to say about negotiation?* Gradually the words *salespeople and their bosses* came to my mind—what would they want to hear? So now, whenever I talk to a VP of sales, I say: "You usually have excellent speakers at your conventions, and they come from a sales background. Would you be interested in me speaking to your salespeople from the customer perspective? You see, I was head of international procurement for a Fortune 500 company. Would finding out the inside secrets of major account-selling help your people? How about dealing with key decision makers in major account selling—would you like an insider to tell you the major mistakes salespeople can make and how to avoid them?" I could go on and on, but you get the message. Become an expert at what you do, and reap the rewards.

- The new gold is not physical—it is intellectual capital.

Ask Unusual Questions

How can you get the critical pieces of information? Learn the art of asking the unusual question. Consider the following story: I have three daughters, Kathryn, Clare, and Anne. I spend a lot of time with them. My oldest daughter is Kathryn, and when she was twelve I said to her one evening, "Kathryn, in what ways could I be a better dad?" Unusual question, isn't it? So I have been told. She said, "Dad, you're very good at taking all three of us out, but I would like just you and me to go out more often." What do you think she was saying? She surprised me with the comment, but the message I took from it was that she wanted more personal attention. So, I swallowed hard because if you do it for one you have to do it for all three.

Over the last few years I have had to go to movies, to rock concerts, and to all those delightful things that teenage girls love to attend. I went to see Rock Bands like 98 Degrees (they were just okay). I went to see 'N Sync and they were terrible. I even went to see the Backstreet Boys in concert at the San Jose Arena, along with 12,000 screaming teenage girls, and they just about knocked my socks off—they put on a great show. Occasionally, you experience the magic.

Anyway, on with the story. When Kathryn was almost thirteen, I had another chat: "Kathryn, you will be thirteen soon, and that's special. You are the first teenager in the family. Why don't you think about how you would like to celebrate it, and we can discuss it in the next few weeks." Well, I must have let the genie out of the bottle when I asked her in what ways I could be a better dad.

"Dad, I've been thinking about what you said about becoming a teenager. I know what I want to do, and I know you are going to say no." "Shoot!" "Well, the *Titanic* movie has just come out. I would love to go to Dublin, Ireland, and London, England, for about a week and see the *Titanic* in San Francisco, Dublin, and London. That way I can tell all my friends I saw the Titanic in three cities on two continents in seven days. That's how I'd like to spend my thirteenth birthday!"

The Titanic

After I had collapsed on the floor and ice-cold water was thrown on me to revive me, I began to think about this proposal. I want my kids to have some good experiences with "the old man" as the Irish call their dads. I figured that if we left Friday evening after school, and took in two weekends plus a President's Day Monday, we could go for ten days, and she would miss four days of school—just about the maximum I was comfortable with. Money was no big deal—you can travel from San Francisco to London/Dublin return for less than $1,000 for two at that time of the year. My sister lives in Dublin and Kathryn had already been to Dublin and London twice before this. To make a long story short, I went for it, and off we went for ten days.

I have seen the *Titanic* in San Francisco, Dublin, and London, and if Celine Dion ever forgets the words of *My Heart Will Go On*, I will cue her, no problem. On the day of February 16, 1998, the day of Kathryn's thirteenth birthday, we had breakfast at the Hard Rock Cafe in London. Guess where we had dinner that day? Would you believe the Hard Rock Cafe in San Francisco? Because of the eight-hour time difference, she had a thirty-two-hour birthday. We flew into San Francisco about five in the afternoon, and we were met by my wife and other two daughters. Then we all went to the Hard Rock Cafe for dinner.

A few days later Kathryn said, "Dad, I'll never forget my thirteenth birthday." What is the moral of this story? Learn the art of asking the unusual question and sometimes magic will occur, in life as well as in business.

Confessions of a Japanese Executive

How can you get the critical pieces of information? Learn the art of asking the unusual question. Consider this example from my professional life: I was in Tokyo negotiating with Fujitsu Corporation. We had just signed off on a multi-million dollar deal. I was the rookie on this trip, but with me were two top vice presidents from my company with over twenty years of relationships with Fujitsu. It was Fujitsu who invited us out to a celebratory dinner in the Ginza in Tokyo.

If you ever have to pick up the dinner tab anywhere in the world, make sure it is not in the Ginza in Tokyo. I looked at the menu and the prices and immediately ordered a double scotch to recover from the shock, and I was not paying. There were three of us, and twenty-one of them. If you ever do business in Japan, you will quickly notice that, for every Westerner, there will be five to seven Japanese.

I was seated beside a Fujitsu executive who spoke perfect English. I said, "Suzuki-san, what keeps you awake at night?" "What an unusual question," he replied. "No one has ever asked me a question like that. Let me think about it and I will get back to you later." Later in the evening he said, "Geraghty-san, I have not forgotten your fascinating question. I have the answer—it is the young people of Japan." "What exactly do you mean?" I asked. "Well, when I think of my father, who fought against the Americans in World War II, it was obvious to me and to all who knew him that he had only four values. Here they are in his order of priority—first, country; second, company; third, family; and fourth, himself. However, I have two teenage sons, aged seventeen and fourteen, and for them, the values are the exact opposite of my father's—first, themselves; second, family; third, company; and last, country. That's what keeps me awake at night—the young people of Japan whose values are so different."

Fascinating exchange wasn't it? By the way, do you think I had a slight advantage next time we did business and were negotiating? Of course I had, because we had this fascinating conversation, which both of us was well aware of. Learn the art of asking the unusual question and magic can happen. Remember I said earlier that top salespeople now listen 70 percent of the time and talk only 30 percent of the time. How can they do that? They have mastered the art of asking the unusual question and listening carefully to the answers. How can you get the critical pieces of information when you negotiate? Ask unusual questions.

Key Issue(s)

You always want to know what the exact key issues are whenever you negotiate. You need to know what the key issues are for your side, and what the key issues are for the other side. Why the other side? Because top negotiators always do this. As I mentioned previously, top prosecution attorneys will first prepare the key issues the defense attorneys will use against their client before they prepare their own brief.

I am sometimes asked to offer my advice in negotiations. The first time I did this I was amazed. I asked three executives privately what the top three issues were for their company, expecting they would be singing from the same hymnbook. Turns out they came up with nine key issues. They had not been communicating with each other at all, and each was looking at the negotiation through the prism of their own department. I had to spend a lot of time getting them to agree on the top three issues for their company. No wonder there's lots of confusion when two big companies negotiate. So, first of all, make sure your own side has its own act together. Then you can concentrate on the other side and find out what their key issues are. Remember that key issues can change quickly, just as leverage can change quickly. Keep your eye on the ball, and keep asking the other side about their key issues.

What was the most famous, or should I say infamous, trial of the twentieth century in America? It was probably O.J. Simpson's. What was the most famous trial of the nineteenth century in America? I don't expect you to know. I certainly did not have a clue until I was doing some research recently. It was the *Rock Island Transportation Case*, regarded by many experts as one of the most famous trials of that century.

The Country Attorney

Here's the plot. It was during the 1840s, when the riverboat barons were the lords of all they surveyed. They were the only game in town, as most of the business was done via boats and rivers, over which they had total control. Their gross margins were outrageous. Everything was going along great for the river barons, until they heard that railroads were being built between New York and California. That made them sweat a little because this was competition. Then they got apoplexy when they discovered that the railroad barons were planning to run railroads over big business rivers like the Mississippi. Guess what happened? The river barons said to the railroad barons, "You do this and we'll see you in court!" They saw each other in court, and for three weeks the trial of the century took place. The river barons got the most famous attorney of the day to defend them. His name was William Wead, who came out of retirement for this "last hurrah." Wead had never lost a river case in his illustrious career, and besides, he was a fantastic speaker who usually charmed and mesmerized his audiences, not to mention the juries.

The case went on for three weeks, and it was standing room only, for those lucky enough to see and hear what was going on. Then came the final day and time for the summations. Wead stood up proudly, and for over three hours summarized his case for the jury. When he concluded, there was not a dry eye in the house. He got a standing ovation from the audience, before the judge intervened to say, "Order, order in the court." The riverboat barons snickered and tried to restrain their confidence. "It's a sure thing" one of them was overheard saying to another, "wasn't Wead amazing?"

They looked at the country attorney getting up to start his summary for the railroad barons, and they felt sorry for him. *How can he follow magic like we just heard?* Then an amazing thing happened. The country attorney only spoke for forty-three seconds, and this is what he said: "Ladies and gentlemen of the jury, I want to congratulate Mr. Wead on a brilliant speech. However, Mr. Wead in his brilliant speech has managed to obscure the key issue. The key issue and the only issue for you to decide upon today is simple. We have a river. The river barons have every right to use the river for business, every right to go up and down the river in their boats. We have no objections to that. All we ask for is equal access—up and down the river by boat, over the river by train. Equal access, which I submit to you, is the only issue and the key issue for your consideration. I rest my case." The country attorney then sat down. Guess who won the case?

You're right. The country attorney won the case. Why did he win the case? Because he found out what the key piece of information was and because he was crystal clear in his presentation. You may not know that the name of this country attorney was Abraham Lincoln, who over a decade later became president. Lincoln had an amazing ability to cut to the chase, to find out what exactly was the key issue, and like a dog with a bone, refused to let go. Great negotiators do the same, and so should you.

Another question for you—what was the greatest speech on American soil in the twentieth century? According to the experts, it was Martin Luther King's *I Have a Dream*. It lasted seventeen and a half minutes. What was the greatest speech on American soil in the nineteenth century? According to the experts, it was Abraham Lincoln's *Gettysburg Address*. The amazing thing about that speech is that it only lasted a few minutes—most unusual for that time. In fact, the speaker before Lincoln was a famous orator, who spoke for two hours. His name was Edward Everett. The following day, Everett sent a telegram to the White House saying, "Mr. President. I should be glad, if I could flatter myself that I came as near to the central idea of the occasion, in two hours, as you did in two minutes."

Great speakers and great negotiators cut to the chase and concentrate on the key issues.

Key Points

- The negotiator who has the most leverage is usually the one with the best information.

- Imagine information as a drama with four characters called Leverage, Expertise, Ask Unusual Questions, and Key Issues.

- Write down in order of importance the six most important things you have to do tomorrow.

- Top negotiators leverage information.

- Leverage means making a little do a lot.

- Decide to become an information expert in a small area.

- The American library system is one of the jewels of the world, yet only 3 percent of Americans have library cards.

- The new gold is not physical—it is intellectual.

5

Time

Let me tell you something very important about this amazing character:

- If you understand the power of time and use it, you will become a champion negotiator.

- The more time you take in preparation for negotiation, the more money you end up with.

- Time is the ultimate power. It's the key to the other *powers*.

Negotiation is a process of discovery for the smart negotiator. This takes time, and the more time you take, the more you discover. Negotiation begins days, weeks, months, and sometimes even years before you sit down at the bargaining table. The better you use that time, the better negotiator you will be.

I said that time is the key that unlocks the other powers. The power of information? It's a matter of taking the time to find out. The power of competition and the things that limit the buyer's ability to use the competition? You discover them by investing the time.

The power of risk taking demands time because risks must be recognized and calculated. You can't discover your powers if you don't take the time to look for them. Invest in time, and you will find that nothing pays better dividends. Are you beginning to get the impression that time is important in all negotiations?

Many sellers today are in too much of a rush. The same can be said for buyers. Close the sale, close the sale, and close the sale, they are told again and again. But what good is it closing the sale, if it's a lousy sale? Buyers/sellers have to discipline themselves to slow down. We have to stop, think, and ask the right questions. We have to use time.

As a buyer I used to assume I had all the time pressures in a negotiation. The other side always seemed to be under less stress than I was. When I became more experienced, I smiled at my innocence. Now I like to give the impression I have all the time in the world to put this deal together. Why do I do this? Because I have come to understand that one of the most powerful weapons in my arsenal is time!

Time Can Be Your Best Friend or Worst Enemy

If you use time wisely, you'll be amazed at how you can persuade people to do things for you. Remember that whenever you negotiate, time can be your best friend or worst enemy. Who will ever forget the dramatic scenes on June 17, 1994? The whole country was transfixed. Nicole Simpson had been murdered. O.J. Simpson's attorney friend had read out a note from O.J., which sounded suspiciously like a suicide note. A few hours later, the television cameras pick up O.J. Simpson's Bronco on the Los Angeles Freeway. Another friend, Al Cowlings, is driving the white Bronco, followed by five police cars. He phones police to say, "O.J. is in the back seat with a gun to his head."

The police know that O.J. is suicidal, so there is a trained negotiator with them, in the car immediately following Simpson. The negotiator knows his best friend in this crisis is time. The longer the crisis goes on, the better the chances that an accommodation can be reached. The other police cars are ordered to follow O.J.'s car but not to attempt to overtake it until further instructions. "Right now, time is my greatest ally," said the police negotiator later, "I remind O.J. of the people who depend on him, his children and his family." In the meantime, the other police were instructed to wait it out, to be patient—above all, to not force a confrontation. They do as ordered, and this classical strategy of crisis negotiators, learned in all kinds of crisis situations, works to perfection. Given time, O.J. relents and does not pull the trigger. This is a very dramatic example of time as a powerful character in that drama. However, it is a very good platform to start from, while discussing the role of time in all negotiations, which is what we are now about to do.

The Taxman Cometh

Have you ever noticed how time can be used against you, to do something that other people want you to do? How do you think hotels get their patrons out? Easy—how about: "Must be out by 11:00 AM or pay another day's rate." Do you think it is effective? You bet it is. And, of course, we have the ultimate time motivator for 90 percent of Americans—April 15. The next time you hear any of the following:

"This offer only good for Thanksgiving Weekend."
"This quote only good for thirty days."
"Hurry, this offer ends on…"

Just smile and remember my words to you.

Ten Minutes to Midnight

I must admit I never realized how important timing was in business until I began working in Silicon Valley. I was only a year in the country, and everything was new and exciting, including negotiating. One day at work, I decided to bring my phone records and notes into one of the conference rooms. As a buyer I was trained to take quick notes after all conversations with salespeople. So I took everything into the conference room, which I had all to myself, with nobody to disturb or distract me. I'm not sure what I was looking for, but as I was going through them, I had an epiphany—an "aha" moment—which I have never forgotten. What was it, and why was it so important?

As I was going through my notes, I discovered something fascinating. Salespeople were not very flexible at all during the first twenty-five days of any month, but in the last week of any month they became much more flexible. My notes from salespeople around the 28th or 29th of the month went like this, "Michael, I have good news for you. I just got the okay from my boss to give you an additional 10 percent discount, but this unbelievable offer is only good for the next forty-eight hours." Sometimes on the thirtieth of the month, these discounts went up to 15–30 percent.

After my aha moment, I then went over to my notes from salespeople for the end of any quarter, and lo and behold even more attractive discounts were being offered. You guessed it—I then went to the end-of-year notes from salespeople and found that they were almost trying to give their products away! Moral of the story—pay attention to that powerful character called Time, and make sure you use it to your advantage, or it will certainly be used against you.

Do you know what smart real estate investors do? Let's say a property is for sale, and the broker has a ninety-day listing with the owner. Smart real estate investors don't want to be making bids during the first seventy days—why? Because the owners are not very motivated. As time goes by, and there are only twenty more days before the listing expires, the owners and brokers become very motivated. The investors are using time to their advantage. Remember the first home I bought in America—it had been on the market for a few months, so I was dealing with motivated sellers. That is why patience is one of the great skills in negotiation. Learn to be more patient whenever you do business or whenever you negotiate, and you will be far more successful.

I am always amazed at how few Americans factor in the time character when they negotiate the price of a car or a home. Next time you decide to buy a car, for example, why would you ever buy it in the first twenty-five days of the month, unless you were desperate? Best time to do it is preferably the end of the inventory year or toward the end of the quarter or near the end of any month, as the salespeople are trying to make their quotas. Just like in comedy, timing can be everything. Learn to use it to your advantage.

Salespeople know that buyers have only so much time to get purchase requisitions off their desks, usually two to four days. How do they know this? The smart ones know the end users in the buyer's organization, who tell them, "I sent it over to that Irish buyer two days ago." I would only do this for the big purchase orders, so I would go to my boss and say, "Boss, I have a requisition on my desk, but I am hanging onto it for a few weeks if need be—the salesperson and I are playing chicken. I think I can get a really good discount if I hold on to month's end." Armed with my boss's okay, I would use time to my advantage.

As an example, a very good salesperson from Sun Microsystems had presented me with a bid for $995,000. (For simplicity, assume $1 million). That included a 24 percent discount. I waited, just like Gary Cooper in *High Noon*, and sure enough on the last day of the quarter, the salesperson phoned me and says, "Michael, if we can book this today, my boss has authorized me to give an additional 16 percent discount." I immediately accepted. What did time earn for me? It earned a 16 percent discount on $1 million, which comes to $160,000. Not bad at all.

Remember that whenever you negotiate, time can be your best friend or your worst enemy.

Acceptance Time: The Parable of the Sick Cat

Understand acceptance time whenever you are in the business of persuasion. Here I want to introduce you to another key idea about time in negotiations. The best way I know is to tell you a story—I hope it will give you a feel for the essence of what I'm trying to tell you.

Consider the spinster who lived with her cat for twenty years, never taking a vacation for fear of leaving her feline companion behind. At a local family gathering to celebrate her sixtieth birthday, her favorite nephew convinced her that her cat would be safe and in very good hands, if she would only relax and enjoy herself on a well-deserved European vacation. She was delighted with this suggestion, and four weeks later her nephew waved her goodbye at the airport, and listened to all her last-minute instructions as to how best care for her beloved cat in her absence.

Tragically, within three days of her departure, the cat ran in front of a car and was killed instantly. The nephew, realizing his aunt would drop dead of a heart attack should she be suddenly told of her cat's demise, created an alternative plan.

The next day when his aunt called home from France, she was told the cat spent the night out in the rain and caught a cold. From England, two days later, she was told the cat was being taken to the vet for shots to cure the very bad cough and congestion. From Italy, word arrived that her pet had been admitted to the animal hospital with pneumonia. From Greece, the message told her that the cat was failing. Finally, while in Switzerland, she was told the cat had passed away, and was given a beautiful funeral.

What is the moral of this story, and why is it important to you? The moral is that most people will accept just about anything, if you give them time. Very often in negotiations, you are trying to persuade people to give up some of their ideas, and see things your way. Remember, people are very comfortable with their own ideas—their ideas are like a comfortable pair of slippers. You will not persuade them to change their ideas quickly. Allow them time, acceptance time. That is why I say this often—patience is one of the top skills of a master negotiator. Patience pays. Give people time to get used to your new idea.

Twice in my life I have had to give bad news to people. On one occasion I had to tell a twelve-year-old that his mother had just passed away unexpectedly. On another occasion, I had to tell a young wife with three kids, that her husband had been killed in a car crash. I'll never forget the look on her face. "You're lying," she said, "it can't be true." Her first reaction was disbelief, followed by bitterness, followed by anger, followed a year later, by gradual acceptance. It was later I understood the process she went though—I read a classic book called *On Death and Dying*, by Elisabeth Kubler Ross. In the book, she explained that grief is a process—that people go through all kinds of heavy emotions like anger, bitterness, and outrage, before eventually, given time, they get around to acceptance.

One salesman has a big sign on the wall in front of his desk that says: "Befriend Time." It's a constant reminder to him that in negotiation time is his strongest weapon, his most faithful ally. Time can also become your enemy real fast. This is especially true when it comes to deadlines. Think about it—deadlines are the use of time to force actions. Be very skeptical of deadlines because many of them can be renegotiated.

Key Points

- If you understand the power of time and use it, you will become a champion negotiator.

- Invest in time during negotiations and you will find that nothing will pay you greater dividends.

- If you use time wisely, you'll be amazed at how you can persuade people to do things for you.

- Patience is one of the great skills in negotiation. Learn to be more patient when you negotiate and you will be far more successful.

- Deadlines are the use of time to force action. Doubt it? Remember April 15th and the IRS.

- People's ideas are like a comfortable pair of slippers. You will never persuade them to change their ideas until you allow them acceptance time.

- Be skeptical of deadlines—many of them can be renegotiated.

6

Iceberg

People are like icebergs—what you see above the water is not as important as what is going on underneath the water. What's the first thing to come into your mind when I say, "Iceberg?" If I said to you, "Every person you meet is an iceberg," what do you think I mean by that? I always ask these questions in my workshops, and I am always fascinated by the answers I hear. Eventually, after some discussion, the groups come up with the right approaches. The most important thing about icebergs is that you see only what is above the water, about 20 percent. What is below the water, the hidden 80 percent, is much more important. Master negotiators understand this, and plan accordingly. All this takes time and energy and creativity, but if the deal is to be put together, this is critical.

I also call the iceberg character the power of personalization—the power of rapport. If you can identify with the person across the table, and they with you, the iceberg starts to melt a little, trust begins to increase, and a deal can be set in motion. Some people call the iceberg other names, such as relationship negotiation, relationship selling, or relationship persuasion. Let's take you and me as an example. When you bought this book, you probably knew very little about me at the beginning. You and I were like two icebergs, meeting somewhere. If you have gotten to this part of the book, you probably know far more about me and how I think. Hopefully my credibility with you has increased as you have gotten to know me better. That's the iceberg character at work. You have to do the same whenever you do business anywhere.

In summary, all negotiators are people. People are like icebergs. For some, price is the most important part of negotiation. I am here to tell you that this is often not so.

Price is always on the table in negotiation. It almost always appears to be the most important issue, and often appears to be the only issue, but it often is not. If we look at the iceberg, as what the buyer really wants and needs, then the tip—always highly visible—represents price. But the tip, however prominent, is a small part of the whole iceberg.

The 80 percent bulk lies under the surface, awaiting your discovery. It is the job of the negotiator to take the time to discover the overall dimensions of this iceberg. What are the needs, wants, and desires of the people across the table? What would make them happy, so we can put this deal together? The most important thing I want you to remember about this amazing character called iceberg is this:

- If you can make people identify with you when you negotiate, you significantly increase your chances of success.

For now, just remember how important all this is, especially now in the global economy, where relationships are so important. Here is the #1 rule for international negotiators: whenever you are in Rome, you must do as the Romans do! That means that when you do business in America, you must do as the Americans do, and let them take the lead. However, some Americans still want to play American rules in Asia, and they wonder why it fails. In most Asian cultures, the relationships you establish and nurture are absolutely critical for your success. I would much prefer a lousy contract in Asia and a good personal relationship, than a perfect contract and a weak relationship. Why? The answer is that the good relationship will get you over and around any difficulty.

An extraordinary meeting took place in the United States some time ago. Some of the top social scientists, psychologists, and psychiatrists met. They had a fascinating agenda to discuss. They were trying to figure out the psychological DNA of the human person. Based on research and the latest psychological findings, they came up with what they called the "Seven Key Psychological Needs" of any human being. Here they are:

THE SEVEN KEY PSYCHOLOGICAL NEEDS

1. **PEOPLE:**   The old song says it best: "People who need people are the luckiest people in the world." Imagine yourself on a desert island. How would you cope?

2. **MEANING:**
                            Each person must answer the questions:
                            Why am I alive?
                            What can I contribute?
                            What meaning is in my life?

3. **ACCOMPLISHMENT:**
    You need to use your God-given talents to benefit yourself and others.
    Not to do so is to condemn yourself to frustration.

4. **RECOGNITION**:
    We all need genuine praise and encouragement.
    We are like flowers—water us and we blossom.
    No recognition and we dry up, like a raisin in the sun.

5. **SECURITY:**
    We all need an environment where we feel secure.
    We need physical, psychological, financial, and spiritual security.

6. **SELF-ESTEEM:**
    The most misunderstood need of all.
    We each need a terrific mental image of self that says: "I was born to succeed, not to fail. I am destined for greatness and not mediocrity."

7. **SELF-DIRECTION:**
    We need to stand on our own two feet.
    We need to think our own thoughts.
    We need to be ourselves—not somebody else.
    Each of us is unique. The tragedy is that so many of us end up as "imitations."

If enough of these needs are met in our lives, then as night follows day, we will be happy and content. If not enough of them are met, then we will end up unhappy and frustrated.

Omaha Beach

Some years ago I met an old man who had been on Omaha Beach on D-Day in 1945. I shook his hand and said, "Thank you for your service." Then in June 2004, I watched the sixtieth anniversary of that momentous day. I was fascinated.

I discovered that over 9,000 American soldiers died on that day—all of them are buried where they died, overlooking the beaches of Normandy. What did CBS do to make this story significant? First of all they recognized they had a problem—the challenge of over 9,000 soldiers, and how to make a compelling story of it in a five-minute report for the national evening news. The challenge was to make people identify with the 9,000 graves. How did they overcome the challenge? Simple—they used the power of personalization.

They took one soldier's story, and this is how it went. The story started with a woman dying in 1984. Her daughter discovers letters in the attic written by her mother and her father, whom she had never seen. Her father had died at the age of twenty-one on D-Day, on Omaha Beach. A narrator reads some of the letters the soldier had written to his wife during World War II and also reads her letters back to him. They use a split screen with photos of the husband and wife, and the music from the time. They show a telegram from the Ministry of Defense "regretting" the death of her husband. Finally the report shows the daughter kneeling at the grave in Normandy, along with her own daughter. It was very moving and very effective precisely because they personalized it. They made people identify with it.

If you can make people identify with you when you negotiate, you significantly increase your chances of success.

The Personal Relationship Strategy

I am a European with over twenty year's experience of living in America. When I first came to America and worked in Silicon Valley, I was amazed at how few Americans used personal relationships when they do business. "Let's get down to business" seems to be the mantra. Many Americans didn't seem to have time for the personal stuff, which is so important in many cultures, whenever you do business.

Have you ever heard of the three kinds of people?

1. Those who make things happen.

2. Those who watch things happen.

3. Those who don't know what the hell just happened!

To illustrate #3, let me tell you a story of some American real estate agents. In 1983–1985, many Iranians were leaving their native country. Why? The shah had just lost power, the Ayatollah was returning from Paris, and a totally new administration was coming to power. Many of these Iranians made their way to the San Francisco Bay Area. They went to see some American real estate agents. "We want to see some houses," they said. The agents, who didn't understand the Iranian culture or the power of personal relationships in business, took them out to see some homes. The Iranians didn't seem to show much interest, so the agents quickly dropped them, thinking they were just "lookers" who would waste their time.

However, these same Iranians went to other American agents, who were culturally sensitive. They understood that Iranians want to have a personal relationship before they will ever consider a business relationship. "We want to see some houses," they said. "Great—I know a lovely Iranian restaurant, why don't we meet there this Thursday for breakfast?" That Thursday at breakfast the American agent says, "Tell me all about yourself and your country…what brings you to America…how fascinating…do tell me more…" After three or more breakfasts (which some people would consider a total waste of precious time), the Iranians said, "We would now like to look at some houses." They bought and then said to the agents, "We have some friends who also want to buy, and we would like to introduce them to you." The agents did not have to take these new clients out to numerous breakfasts—the trust factor had set in, the personal relationship had been established with one Iranian family, and the networking had begun.

So I am talking here about relationship selling, relationship business, and relationship negotiation. Never underestimate the power of the personal relationship whenever you do business with people for the first time.

Let me now share a story of a person who made things happen. As mentioned, for some years I was in charge of international purchasing at a Fortune 500 high-tech company in Silicon Valley. One day, soon after I got this promotion, a parcel arrived at my home. When I opened it, I was very surprised to find that a sales and marketing vice president had sent me some fascinating copies of articles from the *New York Times*, *Wall Street Journal*, and *Fortune Magazine*. The articles were of Irish interest—an article on the Riverdance phenomenon and Michael Flatley, an article on *Angela's Ashes* by Frank McCourt, an article on the Celtic Tiger from *Fortune Magazine.* On the front was a note saying, "Michael, thought you'd be interested. Cheers! Frank."

I called up Frank a few days later and thanked him. He said something very interesting, "Michael, one thing I learned from my mentor many years ago—he told me, 'It is much more important for you to know something about your customer, than everything about your product.'"

Over the next few years Frank sent me interesting articles about once a quarter. What was he doing, and why was he doing it? He was working the personal relationship, and he was paying attention to the fact that I was European and likely to be impressed with this approach. I was. He was paying attention. He was making things happen. And yes I did send business his way.

Will this tactic work every time? Of course not. But try it and see.

Key Points

- If you can establish and make people identify with you when you negotiate, you significantly increase your chances of success.

- The most important thing about icebergs is this—what is below the water, the hidden 80 percent is far more important than the 20 percent you see above the water. Master negotiators understand this and plan accordingly.

- It is the job of the negotiator to discover the overall dimensions of the iceberg.

- Whenever you are in Rome you must do as the Romans do.

- I would much rather prefer a lousy contract in Asia and a good relationship over a perfect contract and a weak relationship.

- In Asia and many other cultures, relationships rule.

- Key psychological needs include people, meaning, accomplishment, recognition, security, self-esteem, and self-direction.

7

Tactics Used by Master Negotiators

In this chapter you will be exposed to some fascinating negotiation tactics used by world-class negotiators. I must warn you in advance that some of them are not ethical, so you may be surprised at seeing them here. I am not suggesting you use any unethical tactic, but I do want you to be prepared if they are ever used against you. I must also confess that I have significantly changed my negotiation paradigm over the years. When I was a rookie negotiator in Silicon Valley in the 1980s, I was a win-lose negotiator. In order for me to win, you had to lose. It was an easy temptation to fall into because I worked for a powerful Fortune 500 company. I eventually discovered that my paradigm was not smart.

I changed my paradigm from win-lose to win-win. If you leave something for the other side, if you also make the other side look good, if you concern yourself with not only satisfying your own needs but also the needs of the people across the table, you'll be amazed, as I was, at the results. Win-win negotiation is the smart strategy to use, not for any moral or religious reasons, but because it makes smart business sense. It is called enlightened self-interest. In fact when I observe negotiations and I see both sides are somewhat dissatisfied at the conclusion, I know that the negotiators on both sides have done a good job. Conversely, when I see one side doing high fives, and the other side looking glum at the conclusion, I am not at all surprised eighteen months later when the atmosphere turns sour, and the lawsuit begins. America is a very litigious society—business deals go sour and the attorneys are called in. Smart negotiators avoid this. My only exception to the win-win rule is when I am buying a car at the car dealer. Then I declare war—the hostilities begin as I face my "opponent" across the table.

So the strategy is the big picture. What strategy do you want to use whenever you negotiate? I suggest you use the win-win strategy, but you must do what you think best. Beware of people who encourage you to view the person across the table as your "opponent." If you do, you set yourself up to play a win-lose game like I used to do. Instead, see the person as your negotiation partner. Have fun with these tactics—experiment, make mistakes, enjoy your triumphs, and learn from your failures. These tactics will help you in small or huge negotiations.

1. Reluctance

- Play the role of the reluctant buyer or the reluctant seller and see what happens.

Many people are very surprised when I tell them that reluctance can sometimes be a fabulous power tactic in negotiations. Let's explore for a moment the psychology of its power. We all know the concept of reverse psychology—you persuade your young son to do something, by telling him to do the opposite. It works for children—how can it work with adults?

Let's suppose you go into a car dealership, and you are enthusiastic about buying a car. What have you just done? You have given away one of your buyer powers. The salesperson comes along and says, "Isn't this a lovely car? Are you interested?" And you say, "You bet I'm interested." Guess who has more of an advantage—the seller or the buyer? Obvious isn't it? Great negotiators never give away an advantage for free.

Let's change the dialogue. Seller says, "Lovely car, are you interested?" Buyer says, "Not really. I'm just looking around. I may buy a car this month, or this quarter, but only if and when the price is right." Notice how the buyer is playing the role of the reluctant buyer. What is going on inside the head of the salesperson? As a seller you always want to show enthusiasm. As a buyer you never want to show enthusiasm.

Are you beginning to see how certain things you thought were weaknesses can in negotiations become your strength? Many people regard reluctance as a weakness—sure it is in certain situations, but not while you are negotiating. Asians are fabulous at turning seeming strengths into weaknesses. I happen to think that the famous American impatience is a wonderful strength for American business. It makes Americans strong in business, getting things done quickly and efficiently.

However, that same impatience can be made a weakness in negotiations, when you have the famous Asian patience meeting the famous American impatience.

Remember the U.S.-Vietnamese negotiations in Paris in the 1960s? International negotiation experts felt that the Vietnamese outfoxed the U.S. negotiators, who were under intense time pressures. The U.S. negotiators came to Paris and rented a villa for two months. The Vietnamese came and took out a two-year lease! They also spent weeks discussing the shape of the negotiation table.

A good friend of mine owns some properties in San Francisco. He never has them for sale, but sometimes he is asked to sell. "John, that property you own on Clement Street—how much do you want for it?" (John has told me privately that he likes to play the role of the reluctant seller.) "Oh, I wish you hadn't asked me about that property—it's my favorite one. I'm not very interested in selling. Make me a great offer and I might consider it, but I really don't want to sell."

Now let's suppose the buyer really is keen on buying the house. Some people will pay more than they bargained for, precisely because what they want is not available. It is all reverse psychology, and sometimes it works powerfully. Will it work every time? No. But all you need is one time to make it work for you.

- Play the role of the reluctant buyer or the reluctant seller and see what happens.

2. Ginger Rogers & Fred Astaire

Mom was right: "Son, always watch your language because you'll get far more from honey than you'll ever get from vinegar."

One thing I have always noticed about world-class negotiators—they are Fred Astaire & Ginger Rogers when it comes to language. They understand that what you say is important, but how you say it is terribly important. They waltz and dance their way around the English language. I am a winter professor at San Jose State University, and I teach negotiation courses there. Sometimes, I ask students to go to garage sales to practice some tactics. Whatever is on sale they are going to ask for a 50 percent discount, and always use the phrase "Would you consider?" For example, a nice table has a price of $40. Students who are practicing their negotiation skills must do two things—(1) "Would you consider" and (2) "$20?"

They have to report their experiments to the class—invariably they are amazed at how powerful this simple use of language works. They come back boasting about how this works like a charm. Consider what would be likely to happen if a student said this—"$20, take it or leave it." Chances are good that a deal will not happen. Most people appreciate courtesy. Conversely, rudeness can kill many good deals.

The ability to say unpleasant things pleasantly is a terrific skill, isn't it? Some people are great at this, while others are a disaster—they say unpleasant things unpleasantly, and then wonder why there are divorces, breakdowns in relationships, and breakdowns in negotiations.

Here are some other examples of this strategy:

> "Thank you."
> "I appreciate your help."
> "I apologize. I made a mistake and I am sorry."
> "Please forgive me."
> "I need your help in understanding this better."
> "Let me repeat what you said and please tell me if I am wrong."
> "Let me summarize what I think I heard you say."

- Mom was right, "Son, always watch your language. You'll get far more from honey than from vinegar. "

3. "Feel...Felt...Found"

- Here is the template: "I understand how you **feel**...(describe what you see). Other people have **felt** the same way...however, because of (present information), they **found** that..."

You don't have to parrot back exactly what I say, or else you will come across as insincere, but use the template "feel...felt...found," and then speak the language you are comfortable with.

This is a terrific tactic whenever things are getting hot and emotional, or you have to cope with an objection. Emotions are a fact of life. When you are angry and upset, you don't want to be making negotiation decisions. When others are angry and upset, a smart move is to take a time-out, just like they do in the NBA.

The opposing team is on a roll, they have just scored a fabulous three pointer, and the home crowd is going berserk—what do you think the opposing coach does? He/she takes a time-out. Smart coaches always do it, and in similar situations in negotiations, smart negotiators do the same.

Nick Price is a good friend of mine. He now owns his own car dealership in Redding, California. For many years he worked at Cole European in Walnut Creek, California, a dealership specializing in Jaguars. It was Nick who told me all about this great tactic, and how he used it. I was surprised when he told me in 1994 that his salary came to $140,000! Not bad for a car salesman, but remember he is catering to upscale Jaguar buyers. "Michael, I have studied the American male very thoroughly. He comes into my showroom to look at a Jaguar. I always know first-time Jaguar buyers because when they are thinking about some problem, they start gently kicking one of the tires on the Jaguar. That's when I make my entrance." (These amateur buyers don't realize they are about to be exposed to a tiger that is about to pounce.)

"I go over and say, 'Isn't this a beautiful Jaguar?' They say 'Yes it is, but this is my first time thinking of buying a Jaguar, and I'm worried because it is a foreign car, and may take a long time to get parts.' I say immediately, 'I understand how you **feel**...most of my first-time clients have felt exactly like you. However when they got their first Jaguar, and started driving some of their buddies around in it, and their buddies were mightily impressed, they **felt** much better—but what really impressed them was this—do you know we are now online anywhere in the world? In the unlikely event your Jaguar broke down, we can have a part to you anywhere in the world within twenty-four hours. When they **found** that out, the problem was no longer a problem for them.'"

Notice what has happened here. The salesman has heard an objection. Some salesman hear objections from their clients and want to prove their clients wrong—not a smart move because even if you convince them they are wrong, you may still lose the sale.

- Marketing Rule # 1: The customer is always right.

- Marketing Rule # 2: Whenever you think the customer is wrong, reread Rule #1.

I have used this tactic in selling real estate. I live in the San Francisco Bay Area, where house prices are high. The first rental property I sold, the buyers were shocked at the price. What did I do? I used this tactic. "I understand how you **feel**...when I first came to America and bought my home I **felt** even more shocked than you; however, here are three listings of similar homes that have sold in this area in the past six months, and you will **find** that the price I am asking is very reasonable..."

Anytime people get emotional doing business, the chances are good that things can go bad quickly. Smart negotiators cut that off at the pass. The most important thing you have to do is to come up with the key piece of information that will turn the objection of your client, into an opportunity for you to sell your solution.

- Here is the template: "I understand how you **feel**...(describe what you see). Other people have **felt** the same way; however, because of (present information), they **found**..."

#4: The Automobile Tactic

- "I am the Mercedes/Lexus/BMW/Rolls Royce of My Profession."

I am a state instructor for the California CPA Society, and four times a year I conduct workshops for accountants, who meet in nice places like Beverly Hills, Palm Springs, Las Vegas, and San Francisco. One of the problems they ask me about is how best handle the usual objection against high accountant fees. A new client comes into their office to discuss business. Things go well until the subject of hourly fees come up.

Client: "What are your fees per hour?"
Accountant: "$300."
Client: "Oh, my God."

How would you handle this?

One way is to look at the number $300. Many accountants and attorneys like nice, round figures like $200 and $300. We will be discussing the "funny money" tactic later. For now let me say this—$295, seems a hell of a lot better than $300, even though in reality it is only a $5 difference. The buyer *perceives* $295 differently. Smart accountants and smart attorneys use this to their advantage when they are deciding on their hourly fees. Smart real estate agents never say the house they are selling is $400,000, when $395,000 seems much more reasonable.

Let's get back to where we were:

Client: "What are your fees per hour?"
Accountant: "$300."
Client: "Oh, my God."

One approach the accountant can use to counter this is the "feel…felt…found" tactic. "I understand how you **feel**. You feel shocked at what you consider my high fees. Most of my first-time clients have **felt** the same as you, so welcome to the club. However, when those same clients found what I can do, my areas of expertise, they **found** me to be a great bargain. I'm sure you will do the same."

Can you think of any other way you could handle this objection? Here's one way that may be helpful in many situations. What if you said the following to the client?

"I understand how you feel—you feel my fees are very high. [You begin by using the first part of feel…felt…found, and then move on.] Would you like to know why my fees are high? I am a Mercedes/Lexus/BMW/Rolls Royce at what I do. [Choose one car.] Many people want expensive cars at inexpensive prices—they would love to get a Mercedes at Toyota pricing. I don't work like that. Ultimately you get what you pay for with me, just like a Lexus/Mercedes/BMW, you pay for quality and expertise."

If you use a calm, professional, measured tone as you say this to your client, your chances of success are higher. Using the auto analogy is helpful because most people understand exactly what you are saying. As always, whenever we are negotiating fees, we are in the business of persuasion—how do you effectively persuade a client that your "high fees" are in reality quite reasonable? One persuasive approach out of many is to remember:

• Marketing Rule #1: The customer is always right.

- Marketing Rule #2: Whenever you think customer is wrong, reread Rule #1.

So agree with clients when they say your fees are high. You could say, "I see you are concerned about my fees. I agree with you—they are high. Would you like to know why they are so high?" Then calmly and professionally explain why, using the auto analogy. This can often stop them in their tracks. Then persuade them that high fees are the price they pay for your kind of expertise.

Another approach to use might be: "High fees in comparison to what? Do you know what Johnny Cochran charges per hour? The answer is $700. I am a terrific bargain compared to some attorneys."

- Remember Fred Astaire and Ginger Rogers and go dance your way to success with your persuasive language.
- "I am the Mercedes/Lexus/BMW/Rolls Royce of my profession."

#5: Corning Glass Tactic

- Great things begin to happen as soon as you get the prospect involved.

One day the CEO of Corning Glass was studying some sales graphs. He noticed that one salesperson was significantly outperforming all the others. A summons went out to the salesperson to come to headquarters and explain the secrets of her success to the CEO. "Sir, my division sells unbreakable glass to our customers. The first six months I sold, the product moved well, but still I was not satisfied. I kept asking myself how could I increase sales? Finally, I tried an experiment. I got a six-square-inch piece of unbreakable glass, along with a large hammer. During my presentation, I would put the sample right on the desk of the prospect. I would tell the prospect, 'See this sample here in front of you? I am now going to raise this hammer to try and shatter the glass. Are you ready?' The prospect would move away from the desk immediately because he expected some glass to be shattered. I would then raise the hammer and with great force hit the sample. The sample would hold firm and stay exactly the same. The prospect would be amazed. 'Oh, my God, that is fabulous. How much of this can you send me, and how soon can you do it?' I would then write out the order. That, sir, is the secret of my success in sales."

The CEO was thrilled—so thrilled that he insisted that every salesperson in that division do the very same thing. Hundreds of these unbreakable samples and hundreds of large hammers were put in the hands of the salespeople. Sales went through the roof. A year later, the CEO was studying sales graphs to discover that the original salesperson was still way ahead of the others in sales. Once again, she was summoned to headquarters to explain the secret of her success.

"Sir, I knew after our last meeting that you would use my technique to increase sales. I knew all the other salespeople would be doing the same thing as me. So I asked myself this question: is there anything different I can do to increase sales even more? I thought about it a lot, and I came up with this new idea. Everything in the presentation was exactly as it was before. However, I did make one change that proved to be critical for my success. I had just placed the sample in front of the prospect on his desk. I got out my hammer but instead of me using the hammer, I gave it to the prospect to use. He would balk at this, but eventually he would do it. The results were amazing as you can see in the graphs. That is the secret of my success. I got the prospect involved. Great things begin to happen as soon as you get the prospect involved."

Is there any way you can get the prospect involved when you sell?

- Ask the prospect to help you out.

6. Stick/Carrot

- Nobody will ever be persuaded by you unless they believe two things about you: you can reward them or you can punish them—sometimes it may be a combination of the two.

Another way of putting this is to use the stick or the carrot. If somehow you can convince people that you can help them or cause headaches for them, don't you think your chances of persuading them to do as you suggest increase significantly? Think for a moment of the power of highway patrol as they cruise along the freeway—have you ever noticed how everybody's driving improves significantly? Why is this? Simple, just recall the above principle.

I am a Christian, and I have always been intrigued by this question—how can a billion Christians be motivated to do anything? How can you persuade them? Simple, if you understand the principle above. Heaven (the Supreme Carrot) and Hell (the Supreme Stick) are fabulous motivators. "If you do as we urge you to do, Heaven awaits, and if you don't do as we urge you to do, the fires of Hell await!" Amazing things happen when you put it this way. People love to be happy and hate to be unhappy. Therefore, this principle is extremely effective in negotiations. Great negotiators make people happy—poor negotiators make people unhappy. "What's it going to take to put this deal together? What would make you happy?"

Snappy Lube

A few years ago I was driving on a California freeway, not too far from home. Suddenly I heard a weird, ominous noise coming from my gearbox. I knew it meant trouble. Two hours later, the mechanic tells me, "This is going to cost you $950." "Oh my God, you can't be serious." "Yes, I am serious. The main problem is no differential fluid—it's totally dry. That means I have to work around the transmission." I must confess I know very little about cars—my mechanical expertise just about extends to turning on the ignition.

However, I do keep good records. I discovered I had gone to Snappy Lube twice in the previous four months for an oil change. I also discovered I had gone to two different Snappy Lube locations. The invoice for one location mentioned the word differential fluid and that it had been checked as full. *That's interesting, let me look at the invoice from the other location.* I did and discovered that there was no mention of differential fluid.

Within the hour I was on the phone to the manager in that location. "This is Mr. Geraghty. I am a very good customer of Snappy Lube. You can imagine my horror when my car broke down on the freeway. I was towed to a garage. The mechanic just told me the main problem is no differential fluid. I was in your place five weeks ago, and unfortunately the differential fluid was never checked. When might I expect your check for $950?" "Oh, Mr. Geraghty, this could be your problem, not ours." "If it is your problem, do you have the authority to write me the check?" "No." "Who does?" "That would be Mr. Steve Davis, the executive VP of our fourteen locations." "Can you give me his phone number?"

"Mr. Davis, this is Mr. Geraghty. I am a very good customer of yours." Then I repeated almost verbatim, what I had said to the manager. Mr. Davis said, "Mr. Geraghty, I understand you are a very good customer—let me send out my mechanic to check the problem." He did, and a few hours later we are back on the phone again. "Yes, I sent out my mechanic and the differential fluid was part of the problem. However, while it was not checked at our location, you also may bear some responsibility for the problem."

"Mr. Davis, I am a businessman and so are you. My time is precious. I don't want to get my attorney involved—he costs $250 an hour. I don't want to go to small claims court. And I certainly don't want to go to Action Line in the *San Jose Mercury News*." (This is a big metropolitan newspaper with over a quarter million local readers—they love to give publicity to these David (me) versus Goliath (Snappy Lube) stories.

Now what am I doing? Why am I behaving like a shark, sensing blood in the water? I am dealing with a very good businessperson. I am trying to persuade him that I can make his life uncomfortable, that I can cause him headaches. How am I doing this? I am threatening punishment. Allow me to say that if you ever threaten punishment, there are two ways to do it—you can do it directly or indirectly. Notice that here I am doing it indirectly. You increase your chances of success if you do it indirectly.

Let's change the scenario. You know I did it indirectly. What if I did it directly? What if I said, "Mr. Davis, when would you like me to unleash my tiger attorney? He's never lost a case like this." Or "Would Wednesday or Friday suit you to meet at the small claims court in Oakland? I am sure you could fit that into your extremely busy schedule, couldn't you?" Or "I am sure your boss would love to hear about the bad publicity for Snappy Lube in the *San Jose Mercury News*, wouldn't he?"

How do you think this approach would go? Chances are good that it would not go well. You never want to tick people off whenever you do business. If you do, logic goes out the window, and emotion takes over. The downside is obvious here. What if he ends the conversation, slams down the phone, saying, "See you in court"? Great negotiators never allow themselves to get into these kinds of shouting matches. They are only interested in increasing their chances of success while negotiating. You do the same.

But let's get back to the plot where I used the indirect approach. "Mr. Geraghty, I understand. Let me think about it. I want to be fair to you and I want to be fair to my company." Later that afternoon, another phone conversation took place. "This is Mr. Davis. I am sitting at my desk and have very good news for you. I am about to get out my checkbook, and write you a check for $500. I know that will make you happy." I must confess that at these words I said to myself, *Michael, the games are about to begin.* Remember, this is business, this is negotiation—sometime it is a chess game. He has made his move. Now it's up to me to make my countermove. I do. "Mr. Davis, there must be some mistake. You just said you were going to make me happy. When you said that, I assumed you were about to write a check for $950. That's what would make me happy. However, $500 would make me unhappy and I know you wouldn't want to do that, would you?" (Nice countermove, Michael.)

I could not get him beyond $675. Remember in an earlier chapter, I told you about the importance of writing down your negotiation goals—that whenever I negotiate, I always have my three goals in writing. For Snappy Lube I had my three written goals:

#1. $950. (What I would love to get.)
#2. $850. (What I'd like to get.)
#3. $750. (Below this I am doing something, like small claims court.)

When he said, "$675 is my final offer," I said, "Mr. Davis, $750 is my bottom line—there is only $75 separating you and me from small claims court." We settled at $750, provided I faxed him my signature and a promise in writing they would not be held liable for anything else. I did. After he got it, he called me back to say that he had received it and was now writing his check. "Thank you, Mr. Davis. I wonder if you could give me the name and address of your boss. I want to write a short thank-you note telling him I found you very professional, and that you had not lost a good customer." I nearly dropped my pen when he told me the owner of Snappy Lube lives on the beautiful and exclusive 17 Mile Drive in Carmel, California. In case you were worried, Mr. Snappy Lube is doing very well. "Thank you" said Mr. Davis, "I appreciate that. Why don't I enclose three coupons with the check for your next three visits to Snappy Lube?" Those three coupons were worth $30 each. So, now I am almost up to $850. Recall what I said to you and always use it to your advantage:

- Remember the principle: nobody will ever do business with you, be influenced by you, or negotiate with you, unless they believe two things about you: You can reward them and/or you can punish them, and sometimes it may be both.

7. Colombo

- Whenever you negotiate, act dumb and see what happens—it may be a smart move. Act smart and see what happens—it may be a dumb move.

Strange but true when you think about it.

Enter Colombo.

I first started watching *Colombo* thirty years ago in Ireland and became fascinated at how he operated. It was only later I discovered that great negotiators do the same, and they use the Colombo tactic to their advantage. In the first quarter of a *Colombo* episode, a sophisticated killer has just killed someone. He is arrogant, smooth, and smart. You can imagine his surprise when this strange-looking detective comes in to interview him. Colombo acts dumb and the killer is smirking to himself, as he tries to help Colombo understand what happened. He thinks to himself, *Where did they get this idiot? I think I'll string him along but really this is ridiculous to have this idiot trying to cope with a genius like me.* End of first quarter.

During the second and third quarters, the genius is beginning to get nervous, and now we're deep in the fourth quarter. Colombo has been asking some interesting questions—Colombo is beginning to find some inconsistencies. The genius is beginning to sweat just a little, but not to worry—genius will handle Colombo, or so he thinks. Time is now marching on, and it is quarter #4. Colombo returns one more time to question the genius, who is now getting extremely nervous and agitated. He is taking some scotch to calm down, but to the acute observer, his hands are beginning to tremble just a little. Colombo signals that the interview is coming to an end, much to the relief of the genius. Colombo makes his final exit—you can see the relief etched on the worried brow of the genius. Colombo turns around for one last killer question—the genius crumbles, admits he did it, and is led off into the sunset…that in summary is the plot of the very successful Colombo series. Colombo acts dumb and it turns out he is the genius. In many negotiation situations, you should do the same.

Let me share with you some examples of how I have used this tactic in Silicon Valley. My company always had to solicit three bids for any product costing more than $5,000. For products costing several hundred thousand dollars, this is what I would do. Let's say Hewlett Packard came in with a bid of $400,000. I would talk to the HP sales rep in this way, "Look, I need your help on this bid. I'm not long off the boat—as you know I'm just a little ol' country boy from a tiny village in Ireland. I am not an engineer, I am not an accountant, and I am not an attorney. You tell me why this is a good deal for my company because I have to convince my bosses that yours is the best deal. From the legal side, what are the top three reasons by which we are safeguarded? From the engineering perspective, why should we go with you? And very important from the financial side, why it this a good deal for us?"

Observe what is happening here. As a negotiator, I am using the Colombo strategy of trying to place myself in the middle—the middleman, trying to sell HP's bid to my upper management. That is a good place to be if you are a smart negotiator. I am forcing them to persuade me that their bid is the best one for my company, and notice how I am doing it—I am just a country boy, not understanding many things—therefore I need their help. Colombo would be proud of me, I hope.

Act dumb sometimes and see what happens. It may be a very smart move.

Next time you buy a car, try out this strategy and see what happens. Act dumb with the salesperson. "Gee, I know nothing about cars. Tell me why this is a good deal for me." If you are smart, say often, "I don't understand—run that by me one more time." Caveat—Colombo will not work for all situations, so be careful. Remember, you are now a negotiating quarterback. Sometimes, one move works brilliantly in certain situations, and at other times it can turn out to be a disaster. Great negotiators use good judgment, and continually ask this question—which strategy or tactic will work best for me here?

Here is another example of starring in the role of Colombo. I used to buy oscilloscopes from a company in Silicon Valley called Tektronics. The sales rep was great—an engineer who could speak great English and was very clear. One day I said to him, "Keith, I know nothing about oscilloscopes. Please explain to me what exactly they are, as if you were explaining them to a sixteen-year-old." This is what Keith said to me, "Michael, let's say you were visiting a friend in the hospital. She has a heart complaint and is hooked up to one of those heart-monitoring machines—you know the ones that go blip-blip-blip, with lines moving up and down the monitor. They monitor the physical activity of the heart. Well, oscilloscopes work just like that. They monitor the electronic activity going on inside the CPU (central processing unit) of the mainframe computer." After that, I had a great understanding of the product. Some months later, I was doing a presentation for upper management, in which they discovered we were spending almost half a million dollars a year on oscilloscopes. A vice president at the meeting said, "Michael, half a million dollars on these—what the hell is an oscilloscope?" You'll never guess what Michael said? If you guessed I said, "Well, Bruce, if you ever visit a friend I hospital…" go straight to the top of the class.

- Act dumb sometimes and see what happens. It may be a very smart move.

- Act smart sometimes and see what happens—it may be a dumb move.

8. Clare

- Always ask for more than you expect—shoot for the moon and you may hit a star.

Clare is my middle daughter. When she was seven, we were walking hand-in-hand around a new shopping mall. We had just turned a corner, when she jumped up and down, all excited," Daddy, daddy, look at that Baskin-Robbins ice cream store—can I have a double scoop with all the toppings?" What was she doing? She was using one of the oldest tactics in the world built into the DNA of every child:

- Always ask for more than you expect.

- Shoot for the moon and you'll certainly hit a star.

"Absolutely not," said I, with my best impersonation of the judicious dad. Did that stop her? Maybe for a few seconds. "Dad, can I have a single scoop?" (Notice how kids figure out things remarkably quickly. She is saying to herself, *Well, I was going for a home run, maybe a grand slam, but Dad is not going to play ball…now what if I try a bunt toward first base…*At this point in the ballgame, I am under pressure, so I do what smart baseball managers do—the opposing team is on a roll, they have just scored a fabulous three pointer, the crowd is going berserk. It is the perfect time to take a time-out. Hopefully it will stop the momentum. I take a time-out by asking my daughter a question, while I get my act together. "Clare, what is our agreement?"

That stopped her for a few seconds. "Our agreement is you take all three of us (I have three daughters) out for ice cream once a week." (This conversation is now going in the direction I like.) "That's right—we go out once a week—what night is that?" "Tuesday." "Great, and what night is tonight?" "Thursday night." "Clare, you got that right. That's why I can't bring you tonight because it's Thursday night, not Tuesday. Besides, even if I did, and I'm not, you would go home and tell Kathryn and Anne, and I would be in big trouble." *Brilliant, wasn't it?* Mentally I was congratulating myself.

I was totally surprised and shocked when Clare, after a minute or two, suddenly said, "Dad, can we just go in and look?" Understand the conversation—I had said quite a lot of no's. I didn't want to come across as an unreasonable tyrant, and this sudden turn in the conversation caught me totally by surprise. So, in a moment of madness, I agreed. "Okay, Clare—we can go in and look, but we are not buying—do you understand we are not buying?" (But think about it, why oh why would you ever go into an ice cream store just to look? Where was my head, and what was I thinking? See the crazy things we humans do every so often?)

We went in "to look," only to find that a class friend of Clare is inside with her dad eating an ice cream. We start to chat because her dad is a junior league soccer coach, as am I. We are chatting away when I look down and Clare is looking up saying, "Dad, I'll have an ice cream just like Amy's." You'll never guess what happened! I put my hand into my pocket, took out two dollars, and Clare got her ice cream.

I have often asked this question: who are the best negotiators in the world? I hear answers like the Germans, Chinese, English, French, and Americans. In my opinion, kids are the greatest negotiators in the world for two reasons. They don't take no for an answer. What a fabulous skill to have. To a kid, no does not mean no. It only means maybe, and if I try hard enough, chances are good that *maybe* can turn into a yes. The second reason kids are fabulous negotiators is that they are very persistent—they keep on keeping on, and don't get too discouraged easily. So, remember Clare's tactic:

- Always ask for more than you expect.

- Shoot for the moon and you'll certainly hit a star.

  PS: Some negotiators will encourage you to ask for far more than you expect. Be careful here. A very important consideration is your credibility. Stretch too far and your credibility may go down the tubes. If that happens, you will have a hard time rebuilding it.

9. The Nibble

- Surprise them in the last two minutes of the fourth quarter.

"Tiredness makes cowards of us all in the fourth quarter."—Vince Lombardi

Another good tactic to use is one called the nibble. The nibble work best in the last quarter of the negotiation game, preferably in the last two minutes. Do not use it in the first quarter. It works best when the other party has spent some time and energy with you. Verbally the words used with the nibble may be "Oh, by the way, there is one thing I want to ask before we finalize the deal…" The use of the phrase "Oh, by the way" should alert you to the fact that the nibble is on its way to you. It works just like a PS at the end of a letter.

Here is an example of the nibble at work. Some years ago, I was buying a new suit in a nice store in San Francisco. The salesperson was friendly and knowledge-able and had spent about fifty minutes with me as I tried on different suits. So, I am now in the fourth quarter—time to think about using the nibble to my advantage. Finally I decided to buy the suit. The salesperson is wrapping the suit up when I say, "Oh by the way, what color shirt and tie are you going to throw in with this lovely but expensive suit?" (I am looking for a free shirt and tie.)

Now, suppose I had said this at the beginning of the first quarter. "Hey, before we start trying on any suit, what kind of shirt and tie are you going to throw in with it, and I am not paying for the shirt and tie." Wish me luck, but realistically what chance do I have?—very little, because the other party has not invested much time and energy. Timing is everything with this tactic. I am now using the nibble just as the referee is looking at his watch and getting ready to blow the final whistle.

But, to get back to the conversation, you recall my saying: "Oh, by the way, what color shirt and tie are you going to throw in with this lovely but expensive suit?" You can imagine my surprise when the salesperson said immediately, "Oh sir, we don't do that kind of thing in here!" I looked at him closely and found an almost hurt-looking expression on his face. My tactic was failing and flailing in the wind. If you were me, what would you have done? Normally, I would have said, "Oh, really, perhaps Brooks Brothers across the street will do that kind of thing over in their store." Having said that, I would calmly walk toward the exit, hoping the salesperson would call me back, saying, "Hold it, we'll throw in a shirt but no tie." Then I would walk back and try for the tie as well.

However, beside me stands my wife, who normally accompanies me whenever I buy a suit because she doesn't trust my taste in suits—besides, I am color-blind. She hates any hassle when shopping, and I know what she is thinking. So I have a quick decision to make—do I want to be a smart negotiator, or do I want the silent treatment on the way home in the car? I do a quick cost-benefit analysis of the situation and say to the salesperson, "Oh really, where I come from, we do it all the time." I am smiling externally, but internally I am fuming—my brilliantly played nibble at the perfect time has now become a disaster. I try hard to be gracious and concede defeat, but it is difficult. I buy the suit, leave my ego there on the store floor, and do not get the silent treatment on the way home in the car. You win some and you lose some!

However, I wish I could take you by the hand and show you the nibbles I have heard and seen in real estate. In the 1980s, I did a fair amount of investing in real estate in the San Francisco Bay Area. Some Irish friends of mine liked to have me with them while they were closing their deals because they were new to real estate and I had some experience. Here are some nibbles I have heard. I must warn you that these nibbles are not ethical, in my opinion. You may be wondering why I am talking here about unethical tactics—I do not encourage you to use them. I do want you to be prepared when they are used against you. And now back to the story. They are sitting at a table with the owners, signing the final documents when the buyer says, "Oh, by the way, I assume the purchase price includes the refrigerator I saw in the garage." We are talking here about $1,000 refrigerator—the big ones with the double doors, and a lot of bells and whistles. In the blink of an eyelid, $1,000 has just exchanged ownership because the nibble tactic has worked to perfection. It has taken the owners by surprise.

Here's another nibble I heard. (Remember this happened in the 1980s when a computer and printer cost almost $3,000.) We are all sitting at the table, signing the final documents, when the buyer says, "Oh, by the way, I assume the purchase price includes the appliances like the computer and printer I saw in the third bedroom?" Again in the blink of an eyelid $3,000 has just exchanged ownership. Notice how the tactic works best if used in the last quarter, and preferably in the last two minutes of the last quarter. The reason for this is that the success of the nibble is in direct proportion to the amount of time and energy the seller has invested.

What is a good counter tactic to the nibble? How about:

> "You assumed wrong."
> "No, it doesn't."
> "You have got to be kidding." Or, "You are kidding, aren't you."
> "Let me think about it and I'll get back to you."
> "I'll have to run that by my husband/wife."

Probably the best countertactic is to name the tactic with humor.

"You're not using the nibble on me are you? Oh, please!"

"Tiredness makes cowards of us all in the fourth quarter."—Vince Lombardi

10. Las Vegas

- In negotiations, the *perception* of the price can be more important than the actual price.

Take a close look at the following

$99.99	$100
$999.99	$1,000
$9,999.99	$10,000
$99,999.99	$100,000

What is the difference between figures on the left, and the figures on the right? Answer: one lousy, miserable, sniveling cent. Key question—is that how it is perceived? The answer is no. Welcome to the intriguing world of perception and funny money. A few months ago, I spent a delightful few days staying in the Bellagio Hotel in Las Vegas. If you saw the movie *Oceans 11*, with George Clooney and Julia Roberts, you will recognize that it was filmed in the Bellagio Hotel. I enjoyed observing other people play poker and blackjack. Ever wonder why you never see real money in Las Vegas casinos? One table I observed had these coins representing $1,000 each. The players were throwing those coins on the table like they were quarters or Monopoly money. Welcome to the world of funny money. It was like playing monopoly except it was for real. You can use this to your advantage whenever you negotiate, or it can be used against you to your disadvantage. Just be aware of what is going on.

I am constantly surprised when attorneys and accountants who should know better charge $200 per hour, $300 per hour, and $400 per hour. Note that $195 per hour, $295 per hour, $395 per hour seems a hell of a lot better for the client. You may say it's only a lousy $5 more. I agree—it is only $5 more, but that is not the way the client sees it. Start looking at it from the clients perspective and act accordingly.

The same goes for real estate agents, who should know better. I often see houses for sale in San Francisco Bay Area. I see "For Sale—$300,000 / $400,000 / $500,000." If you are ready to say, how about $295,000 / $395,000 / $495,000, then move right up to the top of the class. You are beginning to understand that the price may not be as important as the perception of the price. Private car sellers often make the same mistake. I sometimes see this kind of ad on a car:

Car for Sale—$11,000 / OBO

Can you guess two big mistakes in this simple ad? You're right—make it $10,995 and it looks a much better deal, doesn't it? Also never put down OBO (or best offer). Only amateurs do this. When you put down OBO, you are really telling the world you are not really serious about $11,000. It is way better to put down $10,995 and leave it at that. I often see this ad on television: "Only four easy payments of $49.99, plus shipping and handling?" Notice what they are doing. They are using funny money to their advantage. You'd be surprised at how many people actually think the price is less than $50. For those of us who can still do math in our heads, the price is over $200 of our hard-earned money.

IBM used the funny-money tactic to their advantage. At one time they were selling a lower end server for $225,000. Sounds simple, doesn't it? Let's offer it for sale at $225,000. Smart IBM did not choose to do that. They chose the funny-money strategy. They trained their salespeople to say at the end of their sales presentation, "Well, you have seen our excellent presentation. Marvelous server isn't it? Do we have good news for you! We are offering this server for your enterprise, at the unbelievably low rate of only $9.99 per hour. Incredible, I know, but that is what we offer."

Let's look at these two ways of saying the same thing:

"This server costs one quarter of a million dollars of your hard-earned money" or "We are offering this server for your enterprise at the unbelievably low rate of only $9.99 per hour. Incredible, I know, but that is what we offer." (Remember what I told you about the Fred Astaire / Ginger Rogers strategy, and use it always to your advantage.)

Recently I was up in wine country in St. Helena by Napa Valley. I was in a lovely antique store, looking at a beautiful eighteenth-century French antique cabinet. Now, I had no intention of buying it—I am just "practicing" my negotiating skills. The asking price was $20,000. (Doesn't $19,995 look a much better deal?) I said to the salesperson, "I know you would love to get $20,000 for this, but what is the best you can do for me?" "I can take 10 percent off for you." Now, notice what I have just done. By asking a simple little question, I have taken $2,000 off the price in about ten seconds. That's $200 a second—negotiation skills can earn you a lot of money over the course of a lifetime. I continued my chat with the salesperson, "Thank you, but I assume you think I'm one of these rich Californians—I'm just a little old country boy from Ireland—what's the very best you can do for me?" "If you want to do better, you'll have to talk to the owner."

I approached the owner and quietly said this: "I've just been talking to your very nice salesperson. He's giving me a 10 percent discount, but he tells me you can give me a 50 percent discount (okay, I lied!), if I talk nicely to you. Is this true?" "Well, definitely not 50 percent but I could go up a little from 10 percent. What did you have in mind?"

To make a long story short, I got him up to 25 percent discount. He had come down from $20,000 to $15,000. Now that was as far as I went. Remember, I had no intention of buying—all I was doing was testing. But if I was buying, I would at this stage, use the nibble and the funny money tactic. "Oh, by the way,

I assume you knew I was going to use my American Express card. If I did, that would cost you 3 percent of the purchase price. I am going to pay by check, and I assume you have no problem if I deduct another 3 percent from the price? Isn't that fair and reasonable?—3 percent of $15,000 is $450." Whenever you are buying big-ticket items like this, remember if you use American Express, it costs the seller 3 percent and 2.5 percent if you use Visa or Master Card.

- The **perception** of the price can be more important than the actual price.

11. Henry Kissinger

- "You have to do better than this!"

Probably the most brilliant and controversial secretary of state in America during the twentieth century was Henry Kissinger. One day, during the Vietnam War, he called in one of his top workers and this is what he said, "Nancy, I want you to take two weeks off. I have to make major recommendations to the president and his cabinet, regarding Vietnam. I need your help in doing this, so have a report on my desk in two weeks." Nancy did as ordered, and sure enough, in two weeks she produced a beautiful-looking report and left it in Kissinger's office. Two days later, she goes to her office mail slot to discover her report. Attached to the front of report, there was a note in Kissinger's writing that said, "Nancy, you have to do better than this." Kissinger's initials, HK, in his unmistakable handwriting, were at the bottom of this cryptic note.

Sure enough, Nancy took a few more days off, made alterations, amended many pages, added some further recommendations, and nervously left her new report in Kissinger's office. That evening she rushed over to her mail slot and was relieved to find no report. Next evening the same. Evening after that, no change. She was beginning to breathe easier. Friday evening came, and she found her heart pounding as she saw the report back in her mail slot. There was another note from Kissinger saying, "Nancy, you have to do *much better* than this!!!"

This was Starbucks time. Nancy existed on coffee that weekend—she couldn't eat, she couldn't sleep—she spent all the time working on the report. Monday morning comes, and this time Nancy staggered straight into Kissinger's office saying, "Mr. Kissinger, please, no more of these notes on my report. I can't take any more. Everything I have is now contained in this amended report I am giving you. I put my heart and soul into it. Please, no more notes on the report."

Kissinger smiled at Nancy, took the report, and said, "Well, Nancy, if that's the way you feel, and I believe you, I think it's time for me to start reading your report!" He had never read her report, but Kissinger is a professor, and every professor can tell you that students can always do better.

You'll have to do better than that is often called the Kissinger tactic, but it takes many forms:

"You can't be serious."
"Are you kidding me?"
"You're not even in the ballpark."
"You'll have to do significantly better than this."

Remember, negotiation is often the art of the compromise. The seller wants the highest price possible, and the buyer wants the lowest price possible. Negotiation is often the art of getting the seller to come down in price, or persuading the buyer to come up in price. It is a chess game. The Kissinger tactic is one nice move to make in this marvelous chess game of negotiation. The sellers make their move, "This is the price, and this is what I want." The buyers make their counter-move: "I want a fair deal for both of us, but in order for it to be a fair deal for both you and me, you are going to have to show some flexibility on the price."

- "You have to do better than this!"

12. Silent Sally

- Give them the silent treatment and see what happens.

I first discovered this wonderful tactic in Japan. One night in Tokyo, over some sake drinks, a Japanese negotiator said to me, "Geraghty-san, have you ever noticed something about the Americans? They get very nervous whenever you go silent on them. They don't know how to react—it unnerves them. We often give Americans the silent treatment during negotiations, and it is very effective most of the time. Why don't you try it sometime?"

Whenever I hear a good idea, I try to act on it as soon as possible. About three weeks later, I was back home in California getting ready to hear a pricing bid by a company anxious to do business with Amdahl Corporation. I had practiced this silent tactic beforehand and determined I was going to give them the silent treatment. However, I discovered during practice, that I dared not look them in the eye while I am doing it because I would see the funny side of this and start to smile, and a smile would ruin the tactic.

I want to raise your awareness here of a very important moment in any negotiation. Among the most watched behaviors in any negotiation is when the moment of truth comes, and the sellers say, "The price is—." That causes both buyer and seller to get nervous. Whenever the sellers actually tell you the price they want, remember they will be watching your reaction like a hawk. Therefore be careful how you react, and use it to your advantage

Anyway, the salespeople are sitting across from me—they have just given their demonstration of how fabulous their product is, and the spokesperson looks at me and says as sincerely as he can, "Mr. Geraghty, we are very excited about securing your business. We have really sharpened our pencils, and for Amdahl the price is $500,000." I am aware that all eyes are now on me, while I digest this news, and I am aware they must be a little nervous, so I use this to my advantage.

I immediately go into automatic pilot. I hear the words $500,000, and I immediately look toward the ground. I take off my glasses very slowly, put my hand up to my face as if I was getting a bad headache, and start counting silently, (just as I had practiced it), *A thousand and one, a thousand and two, a thousand and three...*I got to a thousand and eleven when guess what happened? The American "cracked" (just as the Japanese said), saying, "Mr. Geraghty, I know we can do better than that!"

The Japanese negotiator was right—give them the silent treatment and see what happens. Here once again, I want to raise your awareness of the psychology of negotiations. They have just made their move and given the price. They are anxious to see my reaction. My reaction seems to be negative. Observe what happens when my response seems to be negative. What is going on inside their heads right now? Probably they are thinking they are going to lose out in the bid. After all, bids are not an exact science. There is always the *fudge factor*—just in case they come in too low, they add 5–15 percent just in case. Probably what is going on inside their heads is this, *Damn our marketing department—this guy is very upset. We better come down real fast or we'll lose the business.* That is probably the reason the salesperson said, "Mr. Geraghty, I know we can do better than that!"

You are probably saying, "Okay for him, he works for a Fortune 500 Company, where he wields power. But poor little me has very little power whenever I negotiate." Really? You may want to look at your own paradigm when you negotiate. Let's say you are buying a car. You've told the salesperson all you want, and now you say, "Okay, when all the dust settles, what is this car going to cost me?" The salesperson gives you a price. Remember:

• Give them the silent treatment and see what happens

I should of course mention the obvious. American wives have discovered this brilliant tactic in the eternal battle of the sexes. Every woman knows that when all else fails and they want behavior modification from their boyfriends or husbands, all they have to do is give them the silent treatment, and presto, behavior modification kicks in automatically. It only took the men a few thousand years to catch up and adapt the tactic to the business world.

Finally, one caveat. Never use this if you are ever negotiating in Ireland. You can count up to a hundred and more—that Irishman across the table is only thinking about that nice pint of Guinness he's going to have later that evening!

13. FUD

• Do what the politicians do—spread fear, uncertainty, and doubt and see what happens.

• FUD = **F**ear, **U**ncertainty, **D**oubt.

Once again let me say I do not encourage you to use this unethical strategy. I just want you to be prepared if it is used against you. I first discovered this tactic in Silicon Valley. Amdahl had to compete head-on with IBM in the very lucrative mainframe market, where a single lower-end mainframe could cost you $2 million, to a higher-end mainframe costing you $18 million. Our strategy was very simple and very effective—we called it "The Magic 10 Percent Silver Bullet." No matter what IBM priced their mainframes, we would market ours as 10 percent cheaper and 10 percent faster. What do you think smart IBM did when they discovered our strategy?

I have always had the greatest admiration for IBM as a company and as a superb competitor. They got to number one, not by being dumb, but by being very smart. They encouraged their mainframe computer salespeople to use the FUD tactic, and this is how they did it. They would meet with decision makers in large accounts and say, "You know, Amdahl is quite a good company—their technology is interesting. However, Amdahl has not been around for long. Many companies come and go—here today and gone tomorrow. IBM has been around forever—we will always be there for you. Who knows where Amdahl is going to be in five or ten year's time? You can be certain that IBM will be there ten years from now, serving you as we have always done."

Brilliant, wasn't it, and for many companies it worked. What IBM was doing was spreading fear, doubt, and uncertainty inside the minds and hearts of their customers. It is one of the oldest strategies in the world, used by some of the best companies in the world.

Politicians of all persuasions use the same tactic to suit their purposes. Every election year in America, the Republicans try to demonize the Democrats, and the Democrats do the same to the Republicans. "If the Republicans get into power," Democrats say, "terrible things will happen to America. The rich will get richer and the poor will get poorer." "If the Democrats get into power," Republicans say, "your taxes will increase."

- FUD = **F**ear, **U**ncertainty, **D**oubt.

- Spread fear, uncertainty, and doubt and see what happens

14. Barter

- Exchange services for money.

Barter is any exchange of services, some of which may be money. Personal satisfaction can often come in ways much different than money.

Some years ago I was doing business in Monterey, California, one of the most beautiful places in the world. I was staying in the Marriott hotel there and loved it. I went to see the general manager, "I really enjoyed my stay here. You run a great hotel. I would love to come back sometime for a week with my family, but I don't want to pay you any money for it!" Remember I am dressed professionally—I had just given a one-day workshop there and was wearing my power outfit—a charcoal-gray-colored double-breasted suit, blue shirt, red tie, and killer shoes to knock your socks off. The GM looked at me warily, saying, "What exactly do you have in mind?" "I am a professional speaker, and I often exchange services. I'm sure there are times your hotel is not full. You have employees who would love to attend a customer service skills workshop. I would be happy to do it free, if in exchange, you let my family stay here during a time you are not busy. Here are some testimonials from GMs like you."

To make a long story short, the GM said he'd think about it. A week later he called me and we agreed on the deal. I would stay in an empty suite for five days with my family, and in exchange, I would give a half-day workshop on key persuasion skills for customer service.

• Do you have a service you could exchange?

I gave the above example to a chapter meeting of the National Speakers Association of America. About two months later, I received a very nice call from one of the attendees. "Michael, I was intrigued by the Marriott example you told us and adapted it to suit myself. I went to see the top manager of Nordstrom near where I live. I was dressed to kill. 'Mr. Ericson, I have a deal for you to consider—I am a professional speaker, and each year I speak in front of 12,000–15,000 salespeople. I genuinely like Nordstrom, and their philosophy of doing business. If I promise to spend a few minutes talking about Nordstrom at each presentation I do, would you consider giving me five top-of-the-line suits from Nordstrom for the next twelve months?'"

I was thrilled to get this phone call. "Barry, tell me what happened after that."

"Well Michael, to be honest, I wasn't expecting it to work as well as it did. He said he'd get back to me, and like you did, I left him with some testimonials from top salespeople who had attended my workshops. About three weeks later he called me, saying he was interested, and could I come in to see him. I did. He wanted to see what exactly I was going to say about Nordstrom. I showed him and he made suggestions for improvement."

Barter is wonderful, isn't it? You'd be amazed at the bartering I have seen in real estate. Some people don't have all the money needed to close the deal—they might have 70 percent or 80 percent but then offer a car, a service, something else instead of money. You see, great negotiators not only are aware of their financial resources—they are aware as well of their nonfinancial resources. You do the same and have fun.

Each year, I bring students who attend my courses at San Jose State University to visit the famous NUMMI plant in Fremont, California. This is a state-of-the-art facility that manufactures Toyotas and GM cars using the celebrated Toyota Production System. It is a joint partnership between GM and Toyota. About 1,000 cars are built there each day. What fascinated me about the original deal, which cost billions of dollars, was that GM had a huge but empty manufacturing facility in Fremont, whereas Toyota had their celebrated production system. Guess what smart GM did during the original negotiations. You are right—they used old-fashioned barter. They managed to save millions of dollars by saying to Toyota, "Look, we have a huge manufacturing location in Fremont, California. It is very close to San Francisco, the gateway for business in Japan. What if we exchanged this, and use it as part of the deal?" Toyota thought it was a great idea.

• Do you have a service you could exchange?

15. Benjamin Franklin

• Figure out the advantages and disadvantages of the deal and decide quickly.

Let me tell you how this tactic was brilliantly used against me. In 1989, I became head of international purchasing for a Fortune 500 company in Silicon Valley. At one stage during that year, I was flying to Tokyo every eight weeks. The only reason I tell you that is that usually I am not a procrastinator, at least when it comes to business. However, with all these trips, I was procrastinating on a decision. In the middle of my procrastinations, I had this call, "Mr. Geraghty, is this a convenient time for you to talk?" (Notice how great salespeople always preface their remarks with this courtesy—many salespeople call, and never ask this question. I always appreciate courtesy, so build this simple sentence into your opening sentence always.) "My name is Frank, and I'm VP of sales and marketing for my company. Sorry to bother you, but I am under enormous pressure myself from my upper management. We need to have a decision very soon as to whether you will be using our services. Tonight I am taking the red-eye flight to San Jose, and I'll be there through Friday. Would it be possible to meet you to discuss this?" The minute I heard red-eye flight, I said, "Of course, why not come in here tomorrow afternoon about 3:00, and I'll be glad to see you."

Next afternoon, Frank arrived, dressed to kill. This was my first time meeting him, as I usually did business with his sales rep. He reminded me of a male model—not a hair out of place. I jokingly said, "Frank, I understand you have to be back in Nordstrom's window in the city by 8:00, so let's get down to business." Frank laughed heartily. "May I call you Michael, or do you prefer to be called Mr. Geraghty?" (Notice again what great salespeople do—they ask for clarification, especially regarding names. They know the power of using your proper name. You'd be surprised at the number of salespeople who call me Mike, after I have introduced myself as Michael! They are not paying attention. If the client says his name is Michael, do not call him Mike). I tell him I prefer to be called Michael. "Michael, Joan never told me you were Irish because I assume that is an Irish accent. Have you ever heard of a famous American called Ben Franklin?" I like to have fun while I work, so I said, "No, Frank—never heard of Ben Franklin, does he play for the Green Bay Packers?" Frank had a great laugh at that one. "Oh, no, Ben Franklin was one of the smartest men America ever produced. The only reason I mention him is that he did something very useful whenever he had to make a big decision. That may be where you are right now—you have to make a decision to go with my company or to go with the competition. And like Ben, whom I call 'wise old Ben,' if it is the right decision, you want to make it quickly and efficiently—if the wrong decision, you want to make it quickly and efficiently. Ben had a method of doing this—may I share it with you because I believe it may be of assistance to you?" (Notice the Fred Astaire / Ginger Rogers use of language all through this conversation).

What Would Wise Old Ben Do If He Were Me?

With that, Frank goes up to use the whiteboard in the conference room. "Michael, wise old Ben would get a piece of blank paper, just like this whiteboard. He would draw a line straight down the center, and on the top left-hand side he would write a big + (plus), the reasons for going ahead with the decision. And on the top right he would write a big—(minus), the reasons for not going ahead with the decision. So let's go to the plus side, put our heads together, and figure out the top reasons why this is a great deal for your company."

Over the next thirty minutes or so, Frank brilliantly explained the reasons why it was a great deal for us. He was sharp, precise, and crystal clear. As he spoke, I realized I was in the company of a master persuader. He brilliantly explained the reasons why it was a great deal from the financial perspective, the technology perspective, and the legal perspective. Between the two of us, we came up with nine reasons for going ahead with his company.

"And now, Michael, let's go over to the right side of the whiteboard—the reasons for not going with my company. Is there anything *you* can come up with?" (Notice how we were all palsy-walsy when we were doing the plus side. With the minuses, I am out there on left wing on my own—smart move, Frank!). I came up with four reasons against the deal, with absolutely no help at all from Frank.

When I had finished, Frank played his master card. He did **not** say, "Well Michael, it's pretty obvious what you should do, isn't it?" Now most salespeople would not be dumb enough to say this verbally, but their attitude conveys the message. Frank was not taking that road. "Michael, here are the reasons for going with us, and here are the reasons for going with the competition. I will be here in San Jose for the next few days on other business. I really would appreciate it if you can call me by Friday, with your decision. I am sorry to pressure you, as I understand how busy you are, but I am under pressure from my bosses." (Notice how he does not oversell. Many salespeople oversell and are left wondering how they lost the sale.)

I went over to him, and shook his hand saying, "Frank, you have the business. Congratulations." (We had already done the negotiations regarding the cost, so why wait—it was obvious to me what I should do.) "Frank, don't worry about the legal eagles or the purchasing folks, we will take care of that later." The next day I called Frank at his hotel. "Frank, that Ben Franklin tool was brilliant." He laughed and said, "Michael, I have to tell you that Ben Franklin has sent my two daughters to college. It is the only tactic I use to close the deal."

Since then I have used this great tactic many times. Sometimes when I tried to sell a rental house and the buyers were procrastinating, guess what I would say? Or when I was trying to sell a car I was privately selling, guess again what I would do, when the buyers thought the price was too high. As with Elvis, there have been many sightings of Ben Franklin in many different parts of America, courtesy of this wonderful tactic.

• Figure out the pros and cons and decide quickly.

16. McDonald's

• Make them feel they are different and you may have the advantage.

Let me tell you what happened. I love observing body language, and how different cultures communicate. Ever observe a group of Italians saying good-bye at an airport? They are leaving each other for a few weeks, but you would think they were never going to see each other again; they are inconsolable. Ever see how the Germans or the English say good-bye? They are usually more reserved. Well, I once was at McDonalds, and I was observing this distraught mother trying to coax her seven-year-old son to take his shoes off in the play structure. "Johnny, you must take your shoes off," I overheard her saying. Did it work here? Of course not. Johnny was a typical seven-year-old, who had decided he was not going to do as his mom said. "No," says Johnny, "I am not taking off my shoes." And he said it with all the ferocious determination that only a seven-year-old can produce.

As a dad, I am totally bemused by situations like this, especially when it comes to other people's kids. I have been at the checkout counter at Safeway, when my seven-year-old daughter decides she wants candy and has a tantrum when I say no. (Don't you love how stores have candies at checkout for kids to go berserk when they see them?) There is a line of impatient shoppers behind me, and I am trying to pretend that this seven-year-old is not my daughter. So, with the greatest sympathy, I am observing this familiar scene being played out before me. "Johnny, if you want to play in here, you have to take your shoes off. Look at all the other kids—see how all of them have taken off their shoes."

I have some questions for you. What did Johnny do next? If you said, Johnny took his shoes off, you are way too smart for your own good because Johnny did not do that! Johnny first of all looked all around the play structure, and sure enough he saw with his own eyes that the one thing all these kids had in common was that each of them had taken their shoes off. He made the connection. What did Johnny do next? He took his shoes off. The most important question I have for you is this—why did Johnny take his shoes off? Answer—he wanted to be just like everybody else; he did not want to be different.

Notice a very important factor in the human personality—people like to feel they are just like everybody else. Smart negotiators understand this important finding in psychology, and use it to their advantage, whenever they are negotiating. Make sure you do the same.

- Make them feel different and you have the advantage.

You are selling your car. Your asking price is $9,995. (Congratulations, you are not asking $10,000, and you don't have OBO after your price—go straight to the top of the class. I am so proud of you!). A buyer comes along, and says to you, the seller, "the price is outrageous." What can you say? Well, you could start using the "feel…felt…found" strategy to counter this, but no—this time you are in the mood to use the McDonald's strategy, and you say to yourself quietly, "How can I make this buyer feel differently so as to give me some advantage?" How about saying in a very calm tone of voice, "Gee, I just turned down an offer of $9750 because I am firm on my price, and I have two more buyers coming to look at the car later today." What you have just done is this—other buyers don't have a problem with the price—why do you want to be different? Will this work every time? Of course not, but it can be very effective in many situations.

At one stage of my career in Silicon Valley, I was negotiating mainframe software contracts. Usually when I do this, I have to do it by phone. Now I don't like to negotiate on the phone because I am Irish (I am a Celt) and Celts like to see you eyeball-to-eyeball, when they do business. However, you often have to do it by phone. Anyway, I was on the phone with this attorney in New Orleans, Louisiana. There was one clause in our contract that was nonnegotiable for my company. I hate to say it was nonnegotiable, that it was cast in concrete, that there was no flexibility, but that's the way this clause was for us. I was having one hell of a time explaining this to Joan, the attorney from Louisiana. She was giving me a real hard time on the clause, and like the good negotiator that she was, she was not taking no for an answer. As an attorney she was doing her "due diligence" work. Finally I decide to play one of my trump cards in this situation.

I said, "Joan, help me understand where you are coming from. I have explained why this clause is very important for my company, which is a Fortune 500 company. I know it is not important for your company, and the reason I know this is that I have personally negotiated this clause with over seventeen attorneys in different states, all of whom had no problem with this clause." What was I doing here? I was taking Joan into our attorney "playpen "and saying, "Look Joan, all the other attorneys who do business in our "playpen" have all taken their shoes off—why do you want to be different?" The following day, Joan called me to say she was graciously yielding on the clause and would accept it "as is." In this instance, it worked quite effectively.

• Make them feel different and you have the advantage

17. Courtship

• You can say, "I love you," to your customer in a hundred different ways.

Ever notice how important atmosphere is in life? Have you ever been in a romantic situation where you are eating a sumptuous dinner with an attractive woman across the table? The lights are low, the music is soft, the conversation is great, and the wine is fabulous. If you had an experience like this, chances are good you will understand the power of this strategy when it comes to negotiation.

The reason I bring this up is that world-class negotiators instinctively understand the importance of "atmosphere" whenever they do business. Very often in negotiations in Silicon Valley, I will call up someone I am going to be meeting for the first time. Months ahead of time, I will call to start "setting the atmosphere" ahead of time. I may say, "This is Michael. Soon, we will be doing business for the first time, and I wanted to give you a quick call to introduce myself. I understand you have a very good reputation, and I look forward to meeting you." What am I doing here? I am using the candlelight, soft music, romantic dinner strategy. Try it out for yourself and see how it works.

I have a question for you. When you do business with anyone, do you prefer to do business with somebody you are comfortable with, whom you know a little and respect a little, or with somebody you don't know but may be very professional? Chances are good it's with the person you are more comfortable with.

I was recently in a Toyota car dealership in Walnut Creek, California. I couldn't believe what I saw. I saw 187 testimonials hanging on the wall. How did I know it was 187? I actually counted them. Some were hand-written and some were computer-generated. All of them had one thing in common—they described a very pleasant experience that the buyers had in this dealership; they were not pressured; salespeople were very courteous and professional; and they would come back and buy again. I noticed a number of prospective buyers studying some of these testimonials. What do you think was going on inside their heads as they were reading? Why did the owner of this dealership have 187 testimonials hanging on the wall?

I went over to see the general manager of the dealership. "I am a consultant on sales; talk to me about these testimonials—they are brilliant." He beamed and said, "You got that right. These 187 testimonials are like 187 silent salespeople—they are my secret weapons. They work 24/7, never call in sick, never have to go on vacation, and never want worker's compensation. They have sold a lot of cars for me."

What had the seller done? He had created a kind of trusting atmosphere, courtesy of the testimonials. So when I talk about mood and atmosphere, I am not talking about wine and music and romance. I am talking about creating a climate where people feel more comfortable doing business with you. Most people feel uncomfortable doing business in a car dealership. This smart owner understood this and said to himself, *How can I make my customer feel more comfortable in here?* Eureka—testimonials. Brilliant isn't it? No wonder this dealership has the #1 in sales for his region.

• You can say, "I love you" in a million different ways to your customer.

Another way you can do it is to simply say "Thank you." I first learned this strategy from Tom Hopkins, one of the top motivational sales trainers in the business. I attended a workshop of his in San Francisco and knew immediately I was in the presence of a superb professional. He told a wonderful story of his mentor giving him this advice: "'Tom, each day, I want you write out five personal hand-written thank-you notes.' So, each day for the past seventeen years, I have been doing this. By this, I mean each business day, so that means twenty-five each week." Someone from the audience then asked Tom this question, "Tom, hold on here for just a minute. Let me see if I understand what you are saying. You send out twenty-five thank-you notes each week. Multiply that by fifty weeks a year and multiply that by seventeen years. That is an awful lot of notes—how on earth do you know that many people?" "You don't have to know them well," Tom replied. "For example, I may be on a plane between Plano and Dallas, Texas. I meet Philip sitting next to me. We talk. Some hours later, while I am at the airport waiting for a connecting flight, I am writing a note to Philip thanking him for the very enjoyable conversation we had over Texas today. We may never meet again, and we only met once. But I always enclose my business card. It's one of the best and most cost effective ways I know for increasing my business."

The power of gratitude in life and in business is enormous. Tap into it soon, and see for yourself. I am a state instructor for the California Society of CPAs. Many of them are owners of a small CPA business, so I often give them this example of Tom Hopkins. I often ask them to start writing personal thank-you notes to their clients, just thanking them for their business and how much they appreciate it. Some of them have e-mailed me, saying their business has increased significantly as a result. It is so simple and so effective.

- You can say, "I love you" in a million different ways to your customer.

18. Involvement

- If you want to get their commitment, you have to get their involvement.

Very often there will be problems in negotiations for all kinds of reasons. Don't rush in too soon to try to solve the problem by yourself. World-class negotiators rarely do this—they prefer the people concerned to get together and come up with a solution to the problem. They want to get them involved. If you get them involved, you will also get their commitment to solving it.

The place was Limerick City, Ireland, made famous by Frank McCourt's *Angela's Ashes*. The cast of characters included twenty-five seventeen-year-olds, their teacher, and me. Here is how the story developed. I was a teacher and a college vice president at the time. I was up in my office musing about my big promotion, when suddenly a teacher appeared, red-eyed and almost unable to talk. "Noreen, I've never seen you so upset. What's wrong?" "I have just been insulted by one of your students, and I want you to discipline him." I was only six weeks on the job, a rookie. *Dear Abby: What's a man to do?*

On my way down the stairs, I recall myself saying, "What the hell am I going to do? My footsteps echoed along the corridor, as I entered the classroom. The class knew the drill. They knew the teacher had gone up to complain to me. They assumed I would do the usual—give the culprit some punishment, along with the customary expressions of "shock that such a thing could happen in this college." I faced the class much like Napoleon faced his troops at Waterloo. I felt like Daniel, going into the lion's den.

"I don't know any one of you. I am a rookie, just six weeks on the job. I was not present for what happened. All I can tell you is this—Mrs. Lynch has been to my office, and she is very upset over what happened. I am going to give this class twenty minutes to decide what should be done about it. I am going to leave you to take care of this, and the only rule I suggest is this—whatever you decide, even if I disagree with it, I will respect 100 percent. I will be back in twenty minutes to hear your decision."

I could see the shock registering on their faces. I turned around and slowly walked away from the classroom, which was now totally silent. On my way back up to my office I was saying to myself, *This is going to be a disaster. Why didn't I just go down, give the punishment, and be done with it?* Negotiator's remorse had set in. Twenty minutes later, I walked down toward the classroom with the same expectation I was going to see the dentist. I was surprised to hear a lot of heated discussion going on. "Mr. Geraghty," one of them said, "we are going to need more time, maybe as much as half an hour." Once again I made my dramatic exit from the class, promising I would be back in thirty minutes.

Thirty minutes later, feigning confidence, I entered the classroom. "Have you reached your decision?" "Yes." "And what is it?" "We have decided that Stephen is going to apologize to Mrs. Lynch in front of the whole class." (*Michael, I was thinking to myself, you are a genius. This is probably what you would have done.*) I was interrupted from my reverie, when they also said, "And we have also decided that Stephen will be grounded for two weeks." I was stunned. This is a boarding college, where students live in residence. Grounding for two weeks is major punishment—no going downtown, no movies, and no fun. The culprit, Stephen, had no problem with the punishment. Why? When I thought about it, I believe the reason was that his peers had decided the punishment.

I want you to think about this story, and the moral of this story. What is the moral of the story? To me, it was this—whenever you have a problem to solve, if you get the people involved in solving it, your chances of a satisfactory solution to the problem, will be significantly increased. I have used this strategy in different parts of the world, whenever negotiations are getting difficult or likely to break down.

• If you want to get commitment *from anybody*, you have to get involvement.

19. Pedro

• Whenever you use a third party, trust everybody, but make sure you cut the cards.

This strategy is most useful whenever you use a third party to help negotiate. It is basically a cover-your-back strategy. In real estate, for example, whenever a broker recommends a title company, or a lender, or a contractor to you, ask them directly if they get a commission from them. Real estate brokers are supposed to tell you this without being asked, but you'd be surprised at how many do not. They are not looking out for you—they are looking out for themselves.

I hope you will remember this story whenever you use a third party:

Seventy years ago in a small Arizona town, a bank robber entered the bank, placed his saddlebags on the counter, raised his gun, and demanded that his bags be filled with gold. The teller obliged and the robber raced to his horse, leaped upon his trusty steed, and headed south to Mexico. The sheriff formed a posse and headed after the robber, catching him just before the border. But somehow during the chase, the robber had time to hide the gold, and so he didn't have it with him when apprehended.

Once they had him, they discovered that he did not speak English, and no one in the posse, including the sheriff, spoke Spanish. A member of the posse was sent to town to find a translator. He returned two hours later with a local resident named Pedro.

"Ask him where the gold is!" The sheriff demanded of Pedro.
"Señor, donde esta el oro?" Pedro demanded.
"No," the robber responded.
Pedro told the sheriff in broken English, "He does not know, señor."

The sheriff then pointed his shotgun at the robber and told Pedro, "Tell him to confess where the gold is or I'll blow his head off!" Pedro rapidly translated in Spanish the sheriff's demand to the confident robber. Suddenly his confidence weakened and he blurted, "El oro esta en el pozo." ("The gold is in the well.") Pedro then turned to the sheriff and with a smile interpreted,

"Senor Sheriff, the robber says 'go ahead and shoot.'"

- "Trust everybody but always cut the cards."

#20: Pavlov

- People react in predictable ways—use it to your advantage.

Ivan Pavlov was a famous Russian doctor and also a superb researcher. How did he become so famous? He conducted a celebrated study called *The Conditioned Response Theory of Behavior*. First, he studied some dogs and how they behaved. He'd make sure the dogs were very hungry. He would show the dogs a piece of meat and then he would ring a bell. Finally, he observed that the dogs would salivate. This went on for some time. Eventually Pavlov would ring a bell, and the dogs would automatically salivate, even though they saw no food. Pavlov concluded that the dogs had developed a "conditioned response" mechanism. The dogs would hear a familiar bell (stimulus), and consequently the dogs would salivate (response).

What has all this got to do with negotiation? Think of it like this—starting in childhood, you have been conditioned to respond to all kinds of stimuli. Over a long period of time, through repetition and reinforcement, you'd be amazed at how often you go into automatic pilot as a result of a stimulus. Ever see one driver cut off another driver on the freeway? What happened? You are watching Pavlov's theory of conditioned response in action. On the freeway, one driver cuts off the other (stimulus), and the other reacts predictably, by getting angry (response). We usually respond to rudeness (stimulus) in a negative way, by anger and/or sarcasm (response).

Great negotiators are acute observers of human nature, and they can use Pavlov's terrific insight to their advantage. Some win-lose negotiators enjoy being negative toward you because it usually works. They try to intimidate you, make you angry, and confuse you. Why? Because it works to their advantage. World-class negotiators have learned to *delay* the usual response. Most people get mad and lose their tempers but not them. They understand what is being done to them, and they deal with it by delaying the usual response.

During one negotiation, one person across the table was deliberately trying to make me angry. "Is it true," he said, "that most Irishmen are alcoholics?" This had nothing to do with the negotiations and the way he said it made it obvious to me he was trying to make me angry. What would you have done if you were me? I must confess there have been times I have become angry, but not on this occasion. I counted to ten very slowly, and then said, "Are you having a tough day?" I enjoyed the shocked expression on his face, and he quickly moved on to another point.

I have been concentrating on the negative side of Pavlov—negative stimuli followed by negative responses. However, like everything else, it can be taken negatively or positively. What if you concentrated on positive stimuli—what do you think may be the conditioned response from the people across the table? Remember people will usually respond to kindness with kindness, respond to courtesy with courtesy, and respond to win-win negotiating with win-win negotiating.

Gandhi once said: "Be the change you want to see in the world."

Here is a good example of Pavlov at his positive best. A single mom wants to buy a first bike for her firstborn son. She goes down to a bike store and listens to a salesperson explain bikes to her—how their reputation for quality is unrivalled. However, the cost is going to be $475. She decides to go to another bike store, and there she hears the following. "Look, I have sons of my own and naturally, as a mom, I want the best for them. I can sell you an expensive bike, and I will make a good commission on it. However, I believe in the golden rule in selling. I suggest you get the least expensive bike because what usually happens with first-time bike riders is that they have lots of crashes. Let your son crash lots of times on the least-expensive bikes, and then, after he gains experience, I suggest you think of a much more expensive bike."

I have a question for you. If that single mom were you, what do you think would be going on inside your head as you listen to this conversation? You're right—this is an unusual salesperson. This salesperson is in my corner—she is credible and I can trust her. Top salespeople use Pavlov to their advantage because people will predictably respond to this type of salesperson with repeat business.

Every time I negotiate, I always expect to be dealing with people who are ethical, nice, and trustworthy. Am I bitterly disappointed sometimes? You bet I am. Sometimes when we shake hands at the conclusion of the deal, I am silently counting my fingers to make sure I still have all five of them. Here is a little experiment for you to test the validity of this theory of Pavlov's. For the next twenty-four hours, smile at everybody you meet. You'll be amazed, as I was, how many will smile back at you. Thanks Pavlov, for the insights.

• People react in predictable ways—use it to your advantage.

21. The College President

• Find out exactly what they want and help them get it.

One night one of the main buildings of Wooster University burned to the ground. Two days later, Louis Holden, the president of that university went to see Andrew Carnegie. Cutting straight to the chase, Holden said: "Mr. Carnegie, you are a very busy man. I promise you I will not take more than five minutes of your time. Two nights ago, the main building of Wooster University burned down. I want you to give $100,000 for a new one."

"Young man," said Carnegie, "I don't believe in giving money to colleges." Holden answered, "But you do believe in helping young men don't you? I am a young man, Mr. Carnegie, and I am in an awful hole. I am in the business of manufacturing college men from raw material, and now the best part of my plant is gone. You know how you would feel if one of your big steel mills was destroyed right in the busy season."

Carnegie said, "Raise $100,000 in the next thirty days, and I will give you another $100,000." "Can you make that sixty days?" said the president. "Done," said Carnegie. As Holden was walking out the door, Carnegie said, "Now remember, it's sixty days only." "All right sir, I understand," said Holden.

Louis Holden's interview had taken just over four minutes. Within fifty days he had raised $100,000. When handing over his check, Andrew Carnegie laughingly said, "Young man, if you ever come to see me again, don't stay so long. Your last call cost me $25,000 a minute." Louis Holden had shot straight for the bull's-eye. He knew Carnegie's Achilles heel.

Think about the above story. Carnegie, a hard-nosed and superb businessman, was not inclined to give money to colleges. How did Holden "make the sale?" He was able to convince Carnegie by speaking his language. Everybody has a hot button. The college president appealed to Carnegie's hot button, which was helping young men to succeed.

Want to know one of the big secrets of selling anything? Here it is:

• Find out exactly what they want and then help them get it.

22. Competition

• "May I introduce you to your competition?"

When I was trying to buy my first home in America, I knew very little about negotiating, as you will see. One evening, my real estate agent brought me over to see a home. It was absolutely lovely—like a doll's house, everything just perfect in it. There was even the smell of cookies all over it, and all the lights were on even though the sunlight was strong (two old tricks of real estate agents as I discovered later). I fell utterly in love with this house—I was besotted with it. Unfortunately, there were other equally besotted admirers looking at it at the same time. Buyer frenzy erupted. I saw one lover writing his bid on his car in front of the house. My agent advised me that if I wanted it, I would need to go over full asking price. They were asking $135,000

Not to be outdone, I wrote a bid on my car that night for $140,000 and begged my agent to sell my offer to the owners. I was devastated the following day when the bid was rejected because another bid had come in at $143,500. See what buyer frenzy can do when buyers want something, and when there is competition for that something? Now I would never bid in this situation as an experienced negotiator. All the advantages are with the seller, so its time to walk away from the deal.

I never fully understood the real power of this "competition tactic" until I started working in Silicon Valley in 1983. I was just a rookie buyer. Our company policy was that for any bid over $5,000, you had to go out for three bids, from three competing companies, and then based on what the bids were, you awarded the contract. The first time I did this I was amazed at the differences in bids on the same project—some were very high and some were very low.

Remember the *Jack Benny Show* in the 1970s? He would pretend he was very bad on the violin. In many of his shows, the violin would come out, and Jack would play it terribly. In reality he was a very accomplished violinist. Well, as a novice negotiator, the competition became my "violin." Every time a salesperson came within hearing distance, I would get out my violin and play this lyric called "The competition is killing you!" "Look, there's an awful lot of competition for our business. Why don't you give me a quote, but remember I am going out for bids on this with three companies. Each of them is very hungry for the business. You are only going to get one shot at it, so come in with your best one because I am not going out again for lower bids."

I wanted those salespeople to believe that the competition was breathing down their necks. I wanted them, last thing at night before hopping into bed, to be worried about the competition, and first thing in the morning, as they were rubbing their eyes and turning off the alarm, to be worried about the competition. You'd be amazed at how effective it was. Now I must confess that I rarely awarded the bid to the lowest bidder because often the lowest one was usually not the best quality one. However, do you think I was going to reveal this to the salespeople? Not on your life.

How can you use this power/fear of the competition in your life? Next time you buy a car, I suggest this as your dialogue with the sales manager, "I intend to buy a car this month but only if the price is right. This is the model I want, these are the features I want in it, and this is the color. I am going to three dealerships with the very same information. The dealer with the best bid gets my business. Are you interested in being one of the bidders?" Now who do you think is more in the driver's seat if you take that approach? The answer is obvious, isn't it? Yet you'd be amazed at how few people follow this approach. What you are doing here is using the competition to your advantage. Remember, all the strategies we are talking about here can be used either *for* you or *against* you.

Do you remember the Susan B. Anthony dollar? The government had trouble getting rid of them. But in the San Francisco post office, people lined up to buy them. Why? They had put up this sign: "Susan B. Anthony dollars. Limit two to a customer." People felt they were in competition for the product. If you can convince salespeople they are in competition for your product, isn't that a source of tremendous power to you as a negotiator, as well as a very smart strategy?

• Make them sweat strategy—use the power of competition

23. Walk-Away

• Do you have the ability, or skill to walk away from the deal?

The walk-away tactic is useful, especially when you don't want the deal. If the deal is not to your liking, the smart move is to walk away from it. What may surprise you is that when you do want the deal, the walk-away may be your best strategy for getting the deal done.

We all live in a world of ambiguity. Most people are not very comfortable with ambiguity. They prefer order, they prefer certainty, and they prefer to feel safe and secure. Great negotiators have trained themselves to be become very comfortable with ambiguity. Whenever you negotiate, you are not entirely sure how things will turn out.

Sometimes tactics and strategies backfire on you, so you must adapt and be flexible or you die. Tension can abound, as the buyer looks for the lowest price, and the seller looks for the highest price. This explains the power of this walk-away strategy.

Sometimes when I teach at the university, I ask my students to experiment with some of these negotiation strategies. Some go to garage sales and practice the *would-you-consider/half-off tactic*. Others buy a copy of the movie called *The Negotiator* and report back on what they saw. Others must go to a car dealership in their local area. They are not to buy a car—remember they are practicing their walk-away skill. I warn them this may take a few hours, but they are to write down what happens to them mentally, while they are doing it.

The car salesman will do his usual until the moment of truth comes—the cost of the car. "For you, I have an unbelievable low price of $19,995..." I instruct the students that this is the moment of truth, when the salesman mentions the price. That is a tense time for both buyer and seller. And it is also one of the most watched behaviors during any negotiation. Think about it, and you'll find how often you have done it yourself. You are selling your car or your home—notice how tense you become when you mention the price—aren't you watching for the reaction from the buyer? In fact you are watching the buyer like a hawk, trying to figure out if they are happy or unhappy with the price. The same goes for the car salesman. I encourage the students to try to look shocked, shake the head, look at the ground, and say sadly, "We are too far apart. I never thought it would be this expensive." Then abruptly you get up and walk toward the door. The students report back to the class on how they felt while they were doing this and what happened.

The fact is that, sometimes, amazing things happen. Sometimes the salesman says, "Hold it—come back here, and let's discuss this further." The student returns, and they discuss this further, the price is lowered further, and once again the student walks out. If you are a buyer, get yourself into the habit of saying, "The price is too high" no matter what you hear. *The price is too high* plus the walking away make a great tactic to use in certain situations, but remember it can be risky. The sellers may let you walk away, and even if they do, you can always return later to say, "I thought it over, and I am willing to come up a bit in the price." The students are always surprised at how much power they have when they do not have to buy the car. *This is just a game*, they are saying to themselves, *and I am only practicing my walk-away strategy.* So the next time you're:

Buying a car...
Considering a salary negotiation...
Buying a home...

• Consider the walk-away strategy, and see what happens.

24. "Dusseldorf Passes..."

• Not doing the deal may be your smartest move.

In 1997, I attended the National Speakers Convention in Los Angeles, along with 2,000 other professional speakers from all over America. One night we had two excellent speakers making presentations during a long dinner. One was Lou Holtz, the Notre Dame football coach, and the other was Harvey Mackay (author of *How to Swim with the Sharks Without Being Eaten Alive*), who told us a great story, and as best I can remember, it went like this: "I was approached by a group of prominent American businessmen. They were starting a European Basketball League, much like the NBA, and they were looking for twenty sports-nuts like myself, to come up with a quarter of a million dollars. It would be in the form of a nonrecourse loan. They promised great things if I did. They were looking for czars of London, Paris, Rome, Athens—I would be the czar of Dusseldorf, in Germany, and that my company would get great publicity."

"To make a long story short, I decided to go for it. They were delighted. To celebrate their triumph, the organizers decided to have a huge gala dinner in Atlanta, and I, along with the nineteen other czars, were encouraged to bring twenty of our friends. I would be sitting at the top of my table with *'Czar of Dusseldorf'* marked prominently on my place. We arrived and the dinner began. I looked around and saw sitting at the next table, the Czar of Madrid. An hour later, the master of ceremonies began his presentation. 'Ladies and gentlemen, we are here tonight to celebrate an awesome achievement—the start-up of the European Basketball League.' (Huge and prolonged applause.) 'We are now going to go around the tables and ask the czars if they are willing to invest a quarter of a million dollars to be part of this new league.'"

"The MC then looked at table #1 London, 'Is the Czar of London ready to say yes?' All eyes looked at the Czar of London, who proudly stood up and said 'London is in.' Immediately, red and blue balloons fell down from the ceiling, trumpets blared, and the spotlight picked out the Czar of London who was enthusiastically greeted with wild applause. Next came Paris with the very same hoopla, and then came Rome with the same hoopla. At that moment I made an amazing decision—I decided I was not going to go ahead with the deal. I felt in my gut that this was too slick and manipulative. This was going to be very embarrassing. All before me had done as promised. I heard the MC turn to me and say, 'Is Dusseldorf in?' With heart pounding and hands trembling, I said 'Dusseldorf passes.' Consternation erupted. A collective gasp was heard all around me. No balloons fell, no trumpets sounded; the spotlight avoided me like the plague. Guess who laughed all the way to the bank eighteen months later when that whole league went belly-up financially?" Moral of story: Sometimes the best negotiation strategy is to pass on the deal.

How many times have I heard?

"If only I hadn't bought that dog of a property…"
"If only I hadn't invested $20,000 in Enron stock…"
"If only the timing had been better…"

I sure wish I knew this strategy when I was a novice in real estate investing and had just bought a condominium that my broker had persuaded me to buy. I should have known better because the property had a negative cash flow—the monthly expenses were greater than the monthly income coming in. Nobody told me that condominiums are not good investments. Compared to single-family homes, there is very little appreciation, and you have very little control because there is usually a homeowners association with monthly fees. Five years later I got rid of this at a loss. The smart thing would have been to use the *Dusseldorf Passes* tactic.

The world and the Internet are full of get-rich-quick schemes. The next time you feel tempted by yet another peddler singing his/her siren song of getting rich quick, remember two things:

- If it seems too good to be true it usually is.

- "I think I'll pass on the deal."

25. Chicago

- Can you distract them from the main issue?

- Razzle-dazzle (*Chicago*) means red herrings, false trails, and distractions.

Recently in San Francisco, I saw the play *Chicago*. During the play, a murder is committed—it turns out that Roxie has killed her lover. She is caught, is in huge trouble, and gets a top attorney to defend her. The murderer is in a sweat because she knows she did it. The attorney is in no sweat because he has a very effective strategy. He is going to give the jury the old razzle-dazzle defense—red herrings, false trails, and distractions. He explains it all in one of the great songs from the show, "Give them the old razzle-dazzle." In case you think this is a little far-fetched, consider Johnny Cochran at the O.J. Simpson trial—smart Johnny gave them the old razzle-dazzle routine and it worked. If negotiations are not going well for you, can you distract them sufficiently from the real issue? It's called the razzle-dazzle, a red herring, a distraction.

Allow me to tell you a story of how this happened to me. Let me put it this way first. If I told you that I actually paid $500 for a cup of tea, you would be quite right in saying I was crazy. I am embarrassed to tell you it actually happened, and here's how it happened. My family in Ireland decided to buy a new home for our parents. The one they had been living in for forty years was showing wear and tear. So my three sisters and two brothers decided we'd all chip in and get a new home. I was chosen as the negotiator. To make a long story short, I met with the owners, and after a long conversation, I made an offer of 28,750 Irish pounds. I knew instinctively that they were happy with this offer. We were both tense and then just as I thought I was about to hear them say yes, the owner's wife asked if I would like a cup of tea. I accepted and we stopped the negotiation while the cup of tea was being made. Half an hour later, we resumed negotiations, and I finished up offering them 29,000 pounds for the home, which they instantly accepted. That cup of tea was the most costly cup of tea I ever had. It distracted me just as victory was in sight. Don't let his ever happen to you—Yogi Berra was correct—"It's not over till the fat lady sings!"

You can use this to your advantage. When things are not going well, when the other side is on a roll, is there any way you can distract them? That is the beauty of the razzle-dazzle. Eisenhower and the Allies brilliantly used it during the Normandy invasion. They deliberately leaked misleading information to the Germans during World War II. The Germans did not expect the Allies to land in Normandy because it was very risky—other places were far less risky and that is what the Germans expected. The Allies distracted them, and the rest is history.

Suppose you decided to open a new restaurant, and I'm not suggesting you do—it's a hard way to earn a buck as many footballers have discovered. However, you decide to take your chances and you open your new restaurant—how would you go about persuading customers to come and eat at your place? Do you know what some smart restaurant owners do when they open a new restaurant? For the first few months, even though they are not full, they tell half the people who phone in for reservations that they are full for whatever night they are looking for. Why do you think they would do such a thing? Simple—they are trying to create the impression this is a great restaurant. Think about it—it is a very effective strategy isn't it? The people who call in do two things when they hear it is "full," they say to themselves, *this must be a great restaurant* and *I must tell my friends.*

- Razzle-dazzle means red herrings, false trails, and distractions.

26. Higher Authority

- Escalate to a higher authority figure.

In many companies, there is such a thing as signature authority. For example, a manager may be good to sign off on anything up to $10,000; a director up to

$25,000; a noncorporate VP up to $50,000; and a corporate VP up to $100,000. Early on in my career in Silicon Valley, I worked in an open office along with fifty other buyers, so I was exposed to all kinds of strategies as buyers "did their thing" with salespeople. I once overheard the following conversation between a buyer and a salesperson:

Salesperson: "We have really done our homework on this bid for you. We have really sharpened our pencils, and this is the very best I can do—the bid is $57,000."
Buyer: "Damn."
Seller: "You look upset—what's wrong?"
Buyer: "I am upset. I'll tell you what's wrong. I was sure you were going to come in at $50,000 or under. I had already gotten the okay from the vice president. However that vice president is a noncorporate vice president, and she is only good for $50,000. You have come in with $57,000—that means I have now to go to the corporate vice president and wish me luck. We call him Hitler because he is so ruthless. Tell you what, do you want a certain yes for $50,000 or do you want an almost certain no for $57,000?" Guess what the salesperson did? He accepted the "certain" $50,000 and left $7,000 on the table.

I happened to know that the noncorporate vice president was the Hitler, and the corporate vice president was the softie, which makes this use of the strategy unethical. I am not suggesting you use unethical strategies—I want you to be ready when they are used against you. What would be a good answer to this buyer? Well you can do the same in reverse. For example, you could say, "Gee, I understand exactly what you are saying because I only have the authority to give you the $50,000 offer. If it goes over that I have to go back and try to get the okay from our Hitler..." Nice countermove isn't it? Remember, negotiation is always a chess game. One party makes their move and you make your counter-move just as if you were playing chess.

27. Withdraw the Offer

• "I'm so sorry—I'm taking the offer off the table."

You may recall the time I was trying to buy my first home in America. A great friend of my in-laws offered to drive me around San Carlos and show me the area. His name was Larry Sifers, a very nice man. Turns out he had a house he was willing to sell for $135,000. I asked for a termite inspection to be done and found there was a lot of termite work needed on the house. I made a lowball offer of $120,000 on the house. I nearly got a heart attack when one night I got a phone call and Larry was on the line. "Michael, I'm sorry, I am taking that house off the market." I was amazed at my reaction—I now really wanted to buy that house big time. That house was now far more desirable to me because I wanted it and I may now lose it.

"Larry, I hope you were not insulted by my offer. It's very nice house, but it does need some work and I assumed you would be flexible in the price." I talked on and on, but no way was Larry going to sell. "Michael, you are now talking to an unmotivated seller. Sorry. I know you will get a nice one and best of luck to you—no hard feelings on my part, nor I hope on yours." I reluctantly put down the phone. Strange, I have often thought about that conversation and the power of the withdrawn offer.

Why did the house become far more desirable after it became unavailable? I have a question for you to consider. When something you really want becomes unavailable, does it become more desirable or less desirable? If you understand the psychology of human nature, you can use this strategy very effectively. But be careful—this has a major downside. The people across the table may believe you are totally serious, and they go elsewhere. If I were you, I might say, "I am *thinking* of taking the offer off the table," and see what happens

- "I'm sorry—I'm taking the offer off the table."

28. Risk-free

- If you make it risk-free, you'll be amazed at the results.

In many negotiations, risk plays a huge role and is a huge psychological factor. I was head of international purchasing for a Fortune 500 company—the risk factor for me, whenever I decided to go with one supplier rather than the competition, was huge. If I made a bad decision, and the supplier did not perform as promised, I looked really bad in front of my peers and bosses. I am very much aware of the risk factor, and the fear factor, in major accounts.

Know what one smart salesperson said to me once? At the time, I was thinking of changing our supplier of copier machines. The smart salesperson, well aware of the risk factor and the fear factor I've talked about, said, "We're convinced our copiers are the best in the industry because we've tracked our frequency of repair very carefully, both in our own plants and in customer locations. Whatever machine you consider, look into its repair record. We don't believe there are any to compare with ours. Also, be sure to ask about service. We stand behind our equipment; we respond quickly when you need us. So be careful—there are a lot of new outfits in the business who deliver the machine and collect their money, and you never see them again." What do you think I was thinking? That's right—repair and service. I was wondering if it would be riskier to buy from her or from someone else. She had successfully reminded me of the element of risk. I decided to stay with her company.

Remember, it's the salesperson's job to point out the reduced risk of doing business with him/her, and gracefully, the increased risk of doing business with the competition. If I'm a buyer, there are risks I don't want to take, especially if I'm in a large organization. Does this give the salesperson an edge? It sure does. It means you can hold the line longer on your prices. It means you can risk a little more, and so make a better deal. Therefore—my unwillingness to risk is a source of great power to you, the salesperson. You should subtly remind me often of this power.

Want to know how mail-order stores significantly increase their sales? One of the cardinal rules of the mail-order business is to always offer the customer a money-back guarantee. Why do they do this? It reduces the **risk** of buying. One speaker asked me how he could increase the number of people who attended her workshops. I suggested she offer a money-back guarantee to anybody who attends. I gave her the language to use, and here it is: "If for any reason you are not completely happy with my workshop, I will give you your money back, no questions asked." And yes, she increased sales by this simple risk-free offer.

- If you make it risk-free, you'll be amazed at what happens.

29. The Seventeen Camels

- Start asking "What if" questions.

Very often in negotiations, there are all kinds of difficulties and obstacles. Some negotiators never get around these obstacles, while others do. The reason for their success is simple—they ask what-if questions. They are very creative. When you get the chance, listen very carefully to one of the best songs Beatle

John Lennon wrote, not long before he died. The song is called "Imagine." Imagine a world without hate or without war. Imagine a world where all the people agree. Imagine a world where there is peace everywhere. Only a very creative person could have written this song. Master negotiators think along the same lines. They ask what-if-questions.

Consider this story:

A man left seventeen camels to his three sons.

He left half the camels to his eldest son.
He left a third to his middle son.
He left a ninth to his youngest son.

The three sons sat down to negotiate a division of their inheritance,
But could not negotiate a solution
—Because seventeen could not be divided by two or three or nine.

The sons finally consulted a wise old woman.
After pondering the problem, the old woman said:
"See what happens if you take my camel."

So then the sons had eighteen camels.

The eldest son took his half (nine camels.)
The middle son took his third (six camels.)
The youngest son took his ninth (two camels.)

They had one camel left over.

They gave it back to the wise old woman.

Creative negotiators are like rare jewels. In difficult negotiations, they continually ask this question: "What if…" So should you!

• Start thinking of what-if questions.

30. Woo Them

- It pays to woo the prospect each time, every time.

Once in San Francisco, my wife and I entered a well-known restaurant, without reservations. It was called "Stars," and it had a famous chef-owner called Jeremiah Towers. There was a long line of customers waiting for tables. I must tell you I hate waiting in line with a passion. Suddenly the owner-chef, Jeremiah Towers, appeared and said: "I'm sorry about the line. It will be about twenty-five minutes. May I bring you a chair or a complimentary cup of coffee?"

Guess what—my customary impatience vanished like a thief in the night. What is going on here? The owner had wooed us successfully. The power of wooing—that's what was going on here. I assume the owner had learned restaurant lesson 101—even when business is excellent, it's very smart to woo the customer, just as you do when business is bad, or when there is no business at all. The owner made me feel he really wanted my business.

Allow me tell you something very important. Salespeople who work for large successful companies, with large shares of the market, with products much in demand, or who are sole sources for their products, often forget this lesson 101—always woo your customer.

An important part of the power of wooing is the power of work. One smart salesperson wooed me for two years before I gave him any business. I was happy with the current supplier but eventually that supplier forgot to continue wooing. Smart negotiators do the very same—even in situations where they have all the power and leverage. Think back to your courting days, when you wooed your significant other. You made your best impression. Apply that experience to all your negotiations. You don't have to marry your negotiating counterpart, but you do have to woo them.

- Remember it pays to woo each time, every time.

31. Influence the Decision Maker

- Influence the decision maker either directly or indirectly.

I remember it as if it was yesterday. The year was 1997, and my wife was getting ready to celebrate a huge event in her life—her fortieth birthday. For months, I had been getting hints about this "special" birthday, and how a nice car would be a fitting gift for this emotional occasion as she said farewell to the thirties. One Sunday, months before her birthday, I was dragged out on a shopping expedition and brought to a car dealer in Walnut Creek, California. To put more pressure on me, she also brought our three young daughters along.

I was in total shock when I arrived at the car dealer lot, and we all gazed at a Toyota Land Cruiser. The smart salesperson asked if we would like to go for a test drive. Before I could answer, the kids were already running toward the car, and during the test drive, I could hear them talking about the lovely smell of the new car. Everybody, except me, loved the car. I hated it. By the way, the asking price was $62,000. I promised the salesperson that "I needed to think about it" and that I would get back to him.

A few weeks later, I come home from work to discover some lovely photographs of a brand new Ford Expedition on the refrigerator. The dinner conversation that night included a discussion, started by the kids, on what color car I would like to buy for "Mom's birthday?" Then a week or two before the big day, the dinner conversation included an exciting report about a friend of my wife's who had just bought a lovely Ford Expedition for "only" $32,000.

I'm sure you know where this true story is going. The weekend of her fortieth birthday, I am dragged kicking and screaming into the car along with our three daughters, and ordered to drive to a car dealership to "look at" a brand-new Ford Expedition. We came home that day driving a new Ford Expedition. My wife, no slouch when it comes to negotiation, had orchestrated a brilliant negotiation campaign.

What is the moral of the story? Many people think they are the lone decision makers when it comes to negotiation, but John Donne was correct—"No man is an island." Everybody can be influenced by the people around them. In the story, I may have thought I was the lone decision maker but turns out I was not. A question I often ask myself when I negotiate is this—who is the real decision maker and how can I influence them? You should do the same.

- How can I influence the decision maker?

32. Anne

• Divide and conquer.

My youngest daughter's name is Anne, and I think the influence of her two more experienced sisters is beginning to rub off on her when it comes to negotiation. She has just turned eleven, and every so often, she says to me, "Dad, I'll need a check next week for something that is happening in school." This request is usually greeted by a comment from me: "Anne, dads are just ATM machines for daughters."

Recently this exchange took place. "Dad, I need a check for $150 for school. The class is going for a three-day trip to Santa Cruz." I go into automatic pilot about dads and ATM machines, as I write out the check. The following week, this exchange takes place. "Dad, did I tell you last week that the check for $150 was only a deposit? The overall cost is $300. I need a check for another $150." Notice how smart negotiators can sometimes break the bad news down into smaller bites. Which is smarter if you are presenting your proposal to the prospect?—One big check of $300 or two small ones of $150?

• Can you divide and conquer?

33. In Memory of my Mother

• Connect to memory and the results may astound you.

• Memories are made of this.

Some years ago I spent a delightful few days at Notre Dame University in Indiana. I love being in famous universities, and Notre Dame has a remarkable history. I was there to talk to some leaders of the International Union of Bricklayers and Allied Craftworkers, the oldest union in America. As I was entering the hall where I was to speak, I was amazed—the hall was state-of-the-art, including all the high-tech sophistication you could hope for as a speaker. Can you guess what the name of the hall was? It was called the Mrs. Eddie DeBartolo Hall. I discovered that the DeBartolo family had donated $11 million to Notre Dame provided that they named the hall in memory of "our mother."

Think about that for a moment. How would you persuade someone to part with millions of dollars? There are different ways to do that. One very effective way is to appeal to memories. The DeBartolo family had no problem parting with millions of dollars. Why? In the wonderful world of persuasion there are all kinds of ways to persuade people to do things. How much are memories worth?

I live on a beautiful campus in a spectacular location in St. Mary's College, Moraga, about forty minutes from San Francisco. One rich family donated to the college five residence halls, costing millions of dollars. Outside the main hall, this Roman plaque contains this message:

> *These residence halls are dedicated to my father Edward S Ageno. He always provided the guiding light my brother Michael and I needed as we grew up. May God bless all who live in these residence halls.*

- Memories are made of this.

34. Humor

- Jay Leno reigns.

I met Tony Parinello some years ago in California. He's a most interesting man. For years he was one of the top salespeople for Hewlett Packard. He now owns his own small training company. He told me a marvelous tactic he uses to get top executives to return his phone calls. He was telling me how he usually sends out hundreds of sales letters to CEOs. He doesn't know them but he is very persistent. After he sends out two letters to a CEO and gets no reply, he then pulls out all the stops with this fabulous tactic.

Late at night he gets into the voice mail of the CEO and leaves this message: "Hello there. My name is Tony Parinello, and I have written two letters to you with a terrific idea that will benefit your company. I know you are a very busy executive, so this is my last communication with you. Every night before I go to bed I can get down on my two knees and talk to God. Now why can't I talk to you? Please call me at…" (and he leaves a number to call).

The moment he told me the story I knew instinctively that over 70 percent of those CEOs would return the call. CEOs are notorious for not returning calls to people they don't know and who can blame them for that? But here we have a negotiator who has figured out a brilliant way to persuade them to return a call. Why do you think a CEO would return this call and ignore all the others? It's the humor that is the key here. Many CEOs think they are "gods," so when they hear this voice mail, they are probably chuckling and saying to themselves, *I have to give this guy a call. I only wish my salespeople were this creative when they are calling on their prospects. Yeah, I think I'll call him if only to satisfy my curiosity.*

Is there any way you can use humor to persuade somebody? Sometimes when all else fails, humor can get you out some very tight corners.

- Jay Leno reigns.

Index of Tactics

1. Reluctance

- Play the role of the reluctant buyer or the reluctant seller and see what happens.

2. Ginger Rogers / Fred Astaire

- Mom was right: "Son, always watch your language because you'll get far more from honey than you'll ever get from vinegar."

3. "Feel...Felt...Found"

- Here is the template: "I understand how you **feel**...other people have **felt** the same way...however, because of (present information), they **found** that..."

4. The Automobile

- "I am the Mercedes...the Lexus...the BMW...the Rolls Royce of my profession."

5. Corning Glass

- Ask the prospect to help you.

6. Stick / Carrot

- Nobody will ever be persuaded by you unless they believe two things about you; you can reward them or you can punish them—sometimes it may be a combination of the two.

7. Colombo

- Whenever you negotiate, act dumb and see what happens—it may be a smart move. Act smart and see what happens—it may be a dumb move.

8. Clare

- Always ask for more than you expect; shoot for the moon and you may hit a star.

9. The Nibble

- Surprise them in the last two minutes of the fourth quarter.

10. Las Vegas

- In negotiations, the **perception** of the price can be more important than the actual price.

11. Henry Kissinger

- "You have to do better than this!"

12. Silent Sally

- Give them the silent treatment and see what happens.

13. FUD

- Do what the politicians do—spread fear, uncertainty, and doubt and see what happens.

14. Barter

- Exchange services for money.

15. Benjamin Franklin

- Figure out the advantages and disadvantages of the deal and decide quickly.

16. McDonald's

• Make them feel they are different and you may have the advantage.

17. Courtship

• You can say, "I love you" to your customer in a hundred different ways.

18. Involvement

• If you want to get their commitment, you have to get their involvement.

19. Pedro

• Whenever you use a third party, trust everybody, but make sure you cut the cards.

20. Pavlov

• People react in predictable ways—use it to your advantage.

21. The College President

• Find out exactly what they want and help them get it.

22. Competition

• "May I introduce you to your competition?"

23. Walk-Away

• Do you have the ability, or skill to walk away from the deal?

24. "Dusseldorf Passes…"

• Not doing the deal may be your smartest move.

25. Chicago

• Can you distract them from the main issue?

26. Higher Authority

- Escalate to a higher authority figure.

27. Withdraw the Offer

- "I'm so sorry—I'm taking the offer off the table."

28. Risk-free

- If you make it risk-free, you'll be amazed at the results.

29. The Seventeen Camels

- Start asking what-if questions.

30. Woo Them

- It pays to woo the prospect each time, every time.

31. Influence the Decision Maker

- Influence the decision maker either directly or indirectly.

32. Anne

- Divide and conquer.

33. In Memory of My Mother

- Connect to memory and the results may astound you.

34. Humor

- Jay Leno reigns.

8

What Prison Do You Live In?

The theme of this final chapter is prisons. I want to suggest to you that you may be in prison and I want to help you escape. A few years ago I visited the island of Alcatraz in San Francisco and became fascinated by its history. For many years it was home to the most notorious prisoners in American history. Al Capone spent many years there, as did "Machine-Gun" Kelly, and "Baby-Face" Nelson who, on being asked by the judge why he robbed so many banks replied, "Because that's where the money is, your honor." I discovered that no prisoner had ever escaped alive from Alcatraz—many had made the attempt, but the frigid waters and treacherous currents of the San Francisco Bay prevented them from reaching land. I looked out from that prison and saw beautiful sights of one of the most beautiful cities in the world and reflected on the irony—prisoners able to observe the city from the prison but never able to visit it.

What prison do you live in? Many people live in prisons far more powerful than Alcatraz. I am not talking here of physical prisons like Alcatraz with prison cells, watching guards, and treacherous currents. I am talking of the "prisons" many people live in. The prison of:

- Low self-esteem.

- A job that you hate.

- A relationship going nowhere.

- A life with no dream or goals.

Add in your own prison by asking yourself, *what prison do I live in?*

In my younger life I had myself in "prison" for at least five years. I had convinced myself that I could never speak in public. That seemed too high a mountain to climb—too deep a river to cross. Anytime I had made the attempt to speak in public, I got heart palpitations, sweaty palms, and dry lips. Like a deer caught in the headlights I got this terrified look in my eyes. And then I decided I had better take this bull by the horns. I decided I was going to conquer this fear.

I also found that Mark Twain was right when he said, "Do the thing you fear and the death of fear is certain." Slowly but surely I overcame my fear of speaking in public, although I found it a long, hard, and arduous process. I got used to speaking in front of five people, then fifty-five, then five hundred, and eventually five thousand. I forget who said this but it is so true: "Yard by yard it's hard, but inch by inch it's a cinch."

Having traveled the world, I have reluctantly come to the conclusion that most people live in some kind of "prison"—they are sleeping giants, unaware of their powers. Social scientists tell us that human beings operate at only 20 percent of their capacity. An image I like is this one—in California, we have beautiful freeways and powerful cars, capable of doing 140 miles per hour, but because of congestion we can only drive those cars at drastically reduced speeds. We are in "prison" with powerful cars unable to perform at peak performance.

I want to summarize one last time what the thesis of this book is. Negotiation is a drama with four amazing characters called Power, Information, Time, and Iceberg. Negotiation is the use of power, information, time, and iceberg to get what you want, and also help other people get what they want. I told you at the start of this book that the more you get to know and understand each of these characters, the better the negotiator you will become. Master negotiators make a lifelong study of these four characters. If you want to become a master negotiator you must do the same—this is the price you have to pay. So, one more time here is my final story to get my point across, and at the same time sum up what this book is all about.

The "Powerless" Prisoner Story

Come with me in your imagination over to San Quentin Prison, overlooking the spectacular San Francisco Bay in California. We are both observing a scene as it plays itself out. A prisoner is pacing up and down his ten-by-fourteen-foot cell. He is restless, like a caged tiger. He remembers his past, in those gray, mean streets of Chicago. He remembers the day he panicked and killed the pregnant woman during that botched bank robbery. He remembers the eyes of the judge as he passed his sentence: "Thirty years—no possibility of parole." His past is bleak. His present is bleak. His future is bleak. Suddenly he stops pacing. He sniffs. The smell is delicious. It's a cigarette. A Camel. His favorite. He shuffles over to the cell door. There, twenty feet away, a guard sits contentedly on a chair, smoking. "God, I'd love a cigarette," says the prisoner. "Get lost!" barks the guard.

Furious, the prisoner paces back and forth, as he mutters to himself, *I have to get my hands on a cigarette. I have to get my hands on a cigarette.* Slowly, relentlessly he plans. Five minutes later he rushes over to the cell door, and this time with authority, he calls over the prison guard. The guard, sensing something different, gets up from the chair and carefully goes near the door. "I want a cigarette, and I want it in the next thirty seconds. If I don't get it in the next thirty seconds, guess what I'm going to do. I'm going to bang my head against this wall until it becomes a bloody mess and I become unconscious. Orderlies will come in, pick me up, and take me out. When I come to, I'm going to swear that you did it. Now you know you didn't do it and so do I, but I'm going to swear that you did it. Think about what will happen. You're going to have to appear before the warden, there's going to be investigations. Reports will have to be made. Now, why don't you give me a cigarette?" Guess what happened? You're right. The guard says to himself, *Do you know what?—this guy may be crazy enough to do it.* The guard does a quick cost-benefit analysis of the situation. Not only did the prisoner get his cigarette—the guard actually lit the cigarette for him.

Let's analyze this story and break it down so we totally understand the psychology behind the story, and the lessons it has for all of us. I like to call it the story of the "powerless" prisoner. The story turns on its head many assumptions we all have about ourselves. Let's look at the first part of the story. Who has the power at the start of story? The guard, probably. The prisoner is "powerless"—he seems to hold no advantage. In fact, all the cards seem to be held by the guard. Plus, the prisoner has no plan. But then something happens to change the momentum. The prisoner decides that he wants something badly enough and plans exactly how he will get it. That gives him power—he uses that power to get what he wants. I have a question for you. Who really had the power in the story? Was it the guard or was it the prisoner? You should know the answer by now.

How many times in your life have you acted just like the powerless prisoner in the first part of the story? You felt the other side had all the power, and you had little or none. *Poor little me* you say to yourself, *is powerless against big powerful them*! You behaved just like the prisoner did at the beginning of the story. I have good news for you—you have far more power than you ever thought you had. That's the lesson I hope you have learned from the story of the powerless prisoner. It's one of the most important lessons you can ever learn in life. I have always believed that most people are sleeping giants, unaware of their powers. This is what this book is all about—alerting you to the great powers inside you. I want to awaken the slumbering giant inside you. Was the prisoner a good negotiator? Was he a good communicator? Did he overcome adversity?

Let's analyze the story further because in the story you will discover again that fabulous model of negotiation, which works for everyone. Let's reexamine for the last time, the PITI model of negotiation.

- Power

- Information

- Time

- Iceberg

Where do you think **power** was in the story? Think about the power of a change of attitude. The prisoner started off with a bad attitude and it got him nowhere. He changed his negative attitude and made it positive. The result? He got what he wanted. You can do the same anytime you want. Think about the power of a plan. He had no plan at the start. The old saying is true: "If you don't know what you want, you probably won't get it." Do you know what you want before you negotiate? Make sure you do from now on.

Do you know what you want from life? From now on, make sure you do.

Think about the power of **information** in the story. The prisoner knew all about life inside prison walls. He understood exactly what guards hate to do—having to go in to the warden's office and explain what happened, the reports to be made out in duplicate and triplicate. The prisoner very effectively used inside information to help him get what he wanted. Information is powerful in all your negotiations. Those who do best in negotiation are those who have the best information. Reread chapter 4 on information and decide to become an information expert in a small area.

Think about the power of **time** in the story. First of all, the prisoner had to spend time in prison finding out the kind of information he would need to get what he wanted.

He also gave the guard only thirty seconds to make up his mind. It worked. Time deadlines are very effective in all your negotiations. Notice how powerful time deadlines are all around us. Time—it can kill us during negotiations, or it can help us win.

"This offer only good for this weekend."

"I can only honor this commitment for 24 hours."

"Do it now, or you'll get a time-out."

Think about the **iceberg** character in the story. The prisoner personalized the threat for the guard. As Don Corleone said in the *Godfather*: "I made him an offer he couldn't refuse." The prisoner brilliantly got inside the head of the guard. He identified with the guard so well that he knew exactly what the guard hated about investigations. If you can make people identify with you, you have the keys of the kingdom.

We all know people who exercise power. Some can do it because their job title gives them power. Presidents and prime ministers are good examples of this. But others, with no job title, also exercise power. This kind of power is fascinating because it is personal power. They wield power by the force of their personality. Power is the ability to influence people or events.

Nelson Mandela is one of my big heroes. He spent twenty-seven years of his life in an African prison, yet even in prison he exercised tremendous personal power. Those who spent time there tell us that even the prison wardens were in awe of the man. If I had to choose between title power and personal power, I would easily choose personal power because it goes wherever you go. Presidents and prime ministers come and go, and so do their title powers.

Research has shown that power is what you think it is. Those who think they have no power negotiate poorly and weakly—even if they do have power. Those who think they have power negotiate from strength—even if they don't really have power. Power is largely in our minds—it's what we think it is!

- If you think you have power, you have it.

• If you don't think you have power, you don't have it.

Your 30-Day Plan to Success

Well, dear reader, we are almost at the end of our journey together. I hope you enjoyed the journey. I have written this book as if you and I were having a drink and a chat in a pub in Galway, on the west coast of Ireland—my favorite place on the planet.

As we say good-bye, consider the fact that you may be in "prison" right now.

If I was given only five minutes to speak to you and I could give you one key to get out of your "prison," and to help you be more successful—here it is. The magic key:

1.   Write down your goals.

2.   Make plans to achieve them.

3.   Work on your plans every single day.

This idea has changed countless lives and it will for you too. Your ability to set goals and work on them every day is the key to your future and your success. Read the book I mentioned already in this book, *How to Get Control of Your Time and Your Life*, by Alan Lakein.

The great oil billionaire H.L. Hunt was once asked the secret of success. He replied, "Success requires two things and two things only. First you must know exactly what it is you want. Most people never make this decision. Second you must determine the price you'll have to pay to achieve it, and then get busy paying that price."

You have a decision to make—do you want to remain in prison or do you want to escape. The choice is yours. I hope you follow the path of the "powerless" prisoner, and the best of luck to you.

May I leave you now with an old Irish blessing.

Irish Blessing

May you live as long as you want,
And never want as long as you live.
Always remember to forget
The things that made you sad.
But never forget to remember
The things that made you glad.

May you live to be a hundred years,
With one extra year to repent!

May your neighbors respect you,
Trouble neglect you,
The angels protect you,
And heaven accept you.

May you have walls for the wind,
And a roof for the rain,
And drinks beside the fire—
May you have laughter to cheer you
And those you love near you,
And all that your heart may desire!

May God be with you and bless you,
May you see your children's children,
May you be poor in misfortune, rich in blessings.
May you know nothing but happiness
From this day forward.

May God grant you many years to live.
May the luck of the Irish enfold you.

Cheers!
Michael Geraghty
Moraga, California, USA.

Key Points

- What prison do you live in?

- Most people are sleeping giants, unaware of their power.

- Decide to make a life-long study of power, information, time, and iceberg.

- I want to awaken the sleeping giant inside you.

- Here is the key to release you from whatever prison you live in.

- Write down your goals.

- Make plans to achieve them.

- Work on your plans every single day.

- May the luck of the Irish enfold you.

About the Author

Michael Geraghty is general manager of Geraghty International Group—a training and consulting company specializing in sales negotiation, conflict management, and executive communication skills. Geraghty is also an executive spiritual coach. He has fourteen years of corporate experience in Silicon Valley, including as head of international purchasing for a Fortune 500 company, for which he negotiated deals and contracts all over American, Europe, and Japan. He is an adjunct professor at San Jose State University and a state instructor for the California Society of CPAs. He is also on the faculty of the American Management Association. Geraghty holds a master's degree from the University of California at Berkeley. IBM has called him "a master storyteller," Oracle calls him "a master negotiator," and Cisco calls him "a delightful speaker." He was featured in Dottie Walter's book, *The Greatest Speakers I Ever Heard.*

His website is www.4irishwisdom.com.
His e-mail address is m4geraghty@yahoo.com.

This book is also available on CD, read by the author.

Also available: *The 10 Commandments of a Successful Entrepreneur*
by Michael Geraghty

For other books and products, see the author's Web site: www.4irishwisdom.com

Michael Geraghty is available for speeches, conventions, workshops, and consulting.

His presentations include:

• Power Secrets of Master Negotiators

• Smart Conflict Management

- 7 Secrets of Successful Speakers

- How to Negotiate in China, Korea, and Japan

Email: M4geraghty@yahoo.com

More Praise for Michael Geraghty

"Thanks for a fantastic presentation to our American and Japanese salespeople. They can be a tough crowd to please and you succeeded with your skillful ability to share personal examples. It was a pleasure having you as our keynote speaker."

—**Will Eckhert,** VP sales and marketing, Shinko Electric America

"Your presentations on sales negotiation skills and building sales relationships was exactly what I think we should see as the path to greatness."

—**Rick Dobbs,** VP sales and marketing, CTB McGraw/Hill

"The Estes Park, Colorado, experience with you on negotiations remains one of those mentally indelible experiences. I do hope we will see you again."

—**Ed White,** regional VP, CTB/McGraw Hill

"A wonderful speaker."

—**Amdahl Corporation**

"Many commented to me about the impact your message had on them. A large percentage of them want you to speak again very soon, which is the sincerest form of appreciation."

—**Robert Korinke,** marketing, IBM Corporation

"The three negotiation seminars you conducted for the National Association of Purchasing Management have been among the highest rated offered by our association."

—**John Semanik**, VP National Association Purchasing Management

Thank you for your workshop on negotiation. You scored very high marks from the forty-seven company presidents both for content and quality. Your insight is extraordinary."

—**P. Rahrig,** executive director, American Galvanizers Association

"Your negotiation keynote in San Diego was excellent. I deeply appreciate your flexibility in being able to substitute at the last minute and give another phenomenal presentation. Requests for your return were among top priorities for next year's conference."

—**Sharon Anderson,** California Environmental Protection Agency

"Your keynote on negotiation at the Mark Hopkins, San Francisco was a gem."

—**National Association of Catering Executives**

"I was very impressed with your presentation and knowledge of negotiation."

—**Julie Velasquez**, president, American Society Women Accountants

978-0-595-36466-4
0-595-36466-7

Printed in the United States
65588LVS00005B/271-309

9 780595 364664